A Voice THAT Kills

A Voice THAT Kills

A REDEEMED STORY OF FINDING
THE **VOICE OF TRUTH** FROM
ABANDONMENT, BROKENNESS, AND AN
UNPLANNED PREGNANCY.

VALERIE MILLSAPPS

A Voice that Kills

ISBN: 978-0-578-82746-9

Psalm 139:16

Valerie Milliapp

DEDICATION

I would like to dedicate this book to the
following people:

My Lord and Savior

I wouldn't be able to write the things I have if it
wasn't for Jesus. He makes all things beautiful
in His time. Thank you for saving me. May I
continue to bring glory to your name all the
days of my life.

Jason

Thank you for always loving me and my crazy
ideas. Your love and support in all that I do
means the world to me. I will never forget the
hard times we faced that made us who we are
today. I know when we face hard times in the
future that God will pull us through.

Cayleigh and Makinze

I am thankful that God sent you both to me.
May you always remember that God sees you
no matter what you go through. May you
always have the courage and boldness to step
into what He has called you to do.

My parents

Thank you for loving me despite my shortcomings and faults. You set a true example of what serving the Lord and hard work looks like. Thank you for raising us up in the way we should go.

My family

I would not be who I am today without your love and support. Thank you for creating special memories that I will always hold dear. I look forward too many more memories we will make together.

My friends

If I named all the special friends that had an impact on my life and still do to this day, I would surely miss someone. Thank you for being that "sandpaper" truth when I needed it. Thank you for pushing me to dream big and help uncover who I was in Christ. Thank you for paving the way to step out and giving me the courage to do the same. I will never forget the moment I sat in the Atlanta convention center and heard a beautiful lady share her desires to serve her local pregnancy center. It was confirmation I needed to trust an unknown future to a known God.

In memory

How I wish that my granny and my uncle Benny were here to experience this incredible moment. May I continue to live a life of significance as I know you would be if you were still here on this earth.

CONTENTS

Dolly Parton and Mannequin Skills

I grew up in the era of Dolly Parton and Conway Twitty. If you know anything about early country music, then you know that these two were pretty much *it*. If you have no idea who I am talking about, I challenge you to take a moment to travel down memory lane and take a listen.

Granny and Papaw knew every word of their songs and I, their little princess, caught on quickly. Granny and Papaw may have been Dolly fans because of her involvement in the theme park, Dollywood. Dollywood is a beautiful theme park nestled in the Great

Smoky Mountains in our great state of Tennessee.

Close to Dollywood, there was a store that had these dresses called "Dolly Dresses." Let me just paint a mental picture for you. Think lacy, poofy, ready-to-enter-a-beauty-contest type dresses. My aunts entered me in one of these beauty contests when I was a baby. I even have an old trophy boxed up somewhere and a picture of me in my Dolly dress.

My two aunts took me everywhere with them. I had, and still have, that sweet southern drawl, the kind you can't help but smile at. In our hometown of Maryville, the beautiful library we have now was once a department store called, "Sky City." There were big red letters across the awning that displayed the store's name. My aunts would frequently shop there and of course, I was right alongside them, twirling around in my Dolly dress. One of these shopping trips with my aunts didn't turn out the way they hoped—they lost me!

They lost me in Sky City!

My aunt Gayle walked all over Sky City yelling for me that day. I loved to twirl in my Dolly dress, but I didn't exactly love to listen. Gayle continued to search for me and yell, "Valerie, Valerie...Answer me please!" She even had the workers searching for me. Finally, they saw me, my sassy little five-year-old self standing perfectly still, like a frozen picture, perfectly posed between two of the store's mannequins.

My aunt Gayle was furious and panicked. She had watched in the movies where children were kidnapped and that was the first thing that went through her mind. She was frantically searching through clothes racks because that was my usual hiding place. She was imagining in her mind how she was going to tell my mom that she lost me in Sky City, and someone kidnapped me. She looked me dead in the eye as I was still in my perfect mannequin pose and asked me why I didn't answer her when she was hollering for me. I cut my big blue eyes at her and tossed my blonde hair over my shoulder and said in my southern drawl, "Silly, I was a mannequin, and mannequins don't talk!" Then I jumped off the platform. Needless to say, she couldn't stay mad at me for very long.

The fear was overwhelming because it was like she was searching for her own daughter, not her niece. That is how much she loved me. This is exactly how Jesus longs for you and I just like this. He desires to have you close. He will seek you out and call your name and run after you because He knows the plans He has for you. He is waiting for you to answer His call. I had a difficult time understanding that. It took a good part of my life before I could say, "Here I am, Lord. Use me however you want." I pray that it doesn't take you as long as it did me. His plans are far greater than we could ever imagine.

If we have asked God into our hearts to save us, He is already involved in our lives. We just have to position ourselves to hear Him speak to us. It is as simple as "practicing the presence of God" and recognizing where He is working in every aspect of our lives, even the simple parts. So, God is there as we load the dishwasher, fold the piles of laundry, type memos behind a desk, or do our homework before school starts.

He has something to say about how we use our finances, how we treat our families or friends, and how we interact with those less fortunate. God is actively working and speaking in every aspect of our lives; we just have to wake up and see Him and open our ears to hear Him. Even when I was running and hiding as a store mannequin, He had me in mind and knew how He was going to use me. He also knows how He wants to use you. All we have to do is say, "Yes."

My Aunt Gayle probably wanted to send me to Jesus that day, but she loved me so much that she was happy to take me back to my mom and dad at our little yellow house.

The Old Yellow House

Growing up, our house was the best. It was on a dead-end street lined with dogwood trees. There was a massive hill as you came down towards our house. This old yellow house nestled on a hill had a big, flat backyard that was perfect for our swing set and an above-ground swimming pool. It was the perfect gathering place where people would either be in the pool or on the swing set.

One side of the swing set was always uprooted from the ground because my sister and I or when my friends would come over, we would try to swing so high that our feet would meet the top of the swing set or higher. You know, the kind of swinging where you would swing so high and so hard that one end of the swing set would come out of the ground and slam back down? I remember the complete freedom and joy of swinging so high, leaping out of the swing, and flying through the air, hoping you landed on your feet. It was a wonder that my sister and I or my friends didn't break an arm or leg flying out of that swing.

The massive hill leading down to our house is where I learned to ride my bike, hands extended in the air. We would hike to the top of the hill and then coast down our dead-end street with our hands flying in the air. We learned how to balance the bike with our legs and do this over and over. There is just something freeing about raising your hands to the sky and flying down that hill on Sunset

Drive. The wind on your face, the smiles, and the laughter I remember so well. It didn't stop with bikes, either. Can you imagine the fun we had when it snowed in the wintertime?

We had the best hill for snow. We would either use the road entrance or many times, we would start at the driveway at our house and fly down the side of the hill to the foot of our neighbor's house. It was always an adventure.

Our little yellow house was *very* 1970s with the green shag carpet in a couple of rooms and brown in some others. My mom said that when they purchased the home, the cabinets were bright orange and my dad had to paint them to tone down the color a bit. He was the cabinet man in our town; he had a gift of creating and refurbishing wood into beautiful things.

Our above-ground swimming pool was a small circle that made for some fun waves. Dad would always make his rounds around the pool to create a huge current that would last forever. When I was eight years old, we were having fun swimming in the pool one day until the side of the pool gave way, sending my dad, sister, and me into the neighbor's yard. It was panic city for a minute as our bodies fumbled about in the gushing water. When the water finally stopped carrying us through the neighborhood like a raft on the river, we all laughed.

One minute you are having fun and suddenly, your world changes can be quite scary. The pool edge breaking, giving way, and the water is rushing you out of the pool and into the unknown. How far will it carry you? Where are we going to end up? You have all these rational thoughts racing through your mind and as the water is carrying you at massive speed you cannot grab ahold of anything. You have no control whatsoever. I was terrified for a moment as this water carried us. Having no control like this pool incident reminds me a little bit about life. We can pick our choices in life but in the grand scheme of things God is in control of our lives. As human beings, we like to have control. When we have no control over what happens, we feel as if we are being pushed down the river with no way to stop. We aren't sure what's next, and that freaks us out a bit. We look for a quick way to come to a fast resolution. What we do not realize is we will look back and laugh and be able to share our experiences about life and how that out of control moment was in the very hand of God, our Creator. He has a plan and purpose for our life.

Isaiah 43:1 (NKJV) says, "But now, thus says the Lord, who created you, O Jacob, and He who formed you, O Israel: Fear not, for I have redeemed you: I have called you by your name; You are mine." God, who created us and formed us, tells us to fear not. Even when you are being carried away by a gush of pool water, fear not. Even when you are being carried away by the trials of life, fear not. What in this life has caused you to fear for tomorrow? What in this life has caused you to fear and worry still today? It was that childlike faith that had me jumping out of high swings and having no fear. It was that childlike faith that had me riding my bike with no hands. Somewhere along the way, something shifts in our mind, and we become captives of the enemy and start to live in fear of our next steps.

Fear takes up camp and robs us of what is true for many years. That stops today. That stops now. My prayer as you take this inside look at my life is that you don't see me, but that you see our Heavenly Father who created you in His image.

In Psalm 139:16 (NKJV) says, "Your eyes saw my substance, being yet unformed. And in your book, they were all written, the days fashioned for me when yet there were none of them." There is some beautiful truth in these words, "my substance, being yet unformed." The Gesenius' Hebrew-Chaldee Lexicon explains it as something that is rolled together.[1] I was not just a budding person of flesh and bone. He saw me as an embryo of the mystical body of Christ. This made me cry when I dove deeper into this scripture.

Scientifically, we know that from the earliest stages of development, an unborn baby is a distinct, living, and whole human

---

[1] Samuel P. Tregelles, *Gesenius' Hebrew-Chaldee Lexicon* (Grand Rapids, MI: Eerdmans, 1964).

being. There is no morally significant difference between the embryo you once were and the adult you are today. God knew you then as an embryo and created you as such, and He knows you now. How amazing is that?! You are fully known and fully loved, and you have always been.

I hope that you will see how you can be free from the lies you believe about yourself and fully walk in confidence in who God created you to be. You can walk fully in God's confidence trusting and anticipating what He will do. You can also see how He can refine us when we make a mess of things. I sure made a few mistakes along the way—still do. He knows even the smallest things we do and loves us anyway.

You Can't Hide Gum from Mom

Grocery shopping with mom was also quite the adventure. Especially for an eight-year-old on a free sample Saturday at the local grocery store. The store would always have little samples to try various kinds of foods, and I would usually go back to the table a couple of times. I am surprised they didn't say "no," but maybe they thought my mom didn't feed me or something.

I got separated from mom at one point and walked past a tall wire bin full of bubble gum. I loved chewing gum, and gum in this big bin was my favorite—the kind that you can blow big bubbles and had great flavor. Before I knew it, I stole a pack of chewing gum. I didn't even think about the consequence at all, just the fact that I wanted a pack of chewing gum. I stuck a pack in my pocket and couldn't wait to get home. I felt a rush of excitement, thinking of chewing that gum, but I also felt a great sense of guilt as I walked away from that tall wire bin. I immediately felt bad and as soon I got home, I hid the gum in my dresser drawer, so my mom wouldn't find it. Right then, with that small act of disobedience in stealing a little ole pack of gum, I became a slave to sin. You are probably thinking, Valerie, that is a little extreme. No, it is the truth.

Taking gum without paying for it was wrong. I knew the right thing to do—pay for it—but I chose not to. Therefore, I sinned. I took it a step further when I hid that pack of gum in my dresser drawer. I would sneak a piece of gum out at a time and chew that gum like there was no tomorrow—until one day my mom saw me and asked me where on earth I had gotten gum. We obviously didn't have any lying around the house. Mom kept asking me until I finally confessed.

If that wasn't hard enough, Mom drove me back to the store with the leftover gum and I had to tell the store employee what I had done. I don't fully remember it, but I imagine myself looking up at the store employee with my sad big blue eyes confessing I, the eight-year-old gum bandit, had taken something that didn't belong to me. Mom paid for the gum and we left.

There is a powerful story here. Maybe you have had a moment like this? Or have gone through something like this? You know that something you have done or thought about doing is wrong and you want to shove it down and hide it so that no one will ever know. You convince yourself that if you keep stuffing it down, maybe one day you will forget all about it. That is simply…NOT TRUE. God's word tells us as much.

Let's dive into the very beginning. In Genesis 1:27 (NKJV), we are reminded that God created man in His own image, "in the image of God He created him; male and female He created them." You were created for a purpose. You may not realize it yet, but you are. You may be thinking, *but you have no idea what I have done in my past. How on earth can*

I really be made for a greater purpose? Adam

and Eve were, and they messed up big time,

but God's mercy covers them. Let's see how,

shall we?

Temptations and the Fall

In Genesis 2, we have a beautiful story that takes place in the Garden of Eden. God placed Adam here in this massive garden. Every tree in this garden was breathtaking to the eye and great for food. In the middle of the massive garden were the tree of life and the tree of knowledge of good and evil. It was in Eden, which signifies delight and pleasure, and a river went out of Eden to water the garden. I can only imagine how beautiful this garden was.

The Lord gave very specific instructions to Adam while he was in the garden. Every tree was absolutely breathtaking. I can picture in my mind how beautiful this moment was. Kind of like standing and looking over the Grand Canyon National Park in Arizona. It is so beautiful and as you look out it doesn't even seem real. So here Adam was overlooking this garden and he couldn't believe what he was seeing. He could eat off any of these beautiful trees of the garden, but this one. It is kind of like a toddler in a toy store. You can have any toy in this store, but not this selection of toys. That toy is off-limits. Adam was told it was "hands-off" this one tree or he would die. He had everything he needed: food, the beauty of this garden, water, shelter, and fellowship with God. What more could you ask for?

But the Lord wanted Adam to have something else—a helper. So, Adam was put in this deep sleep and the Lord took one of his ribs. This rib that the Lord had removed from Adam, he took that and made it into a woman. And in Genesis 2:23 (NKJV) says, "And Adam said: "This is now bone of my bones and flesh of my flesh; She shall be called Woman because she was taken out of man". God made man and woman in His image with physical and emotional needs that only another human being could meet. No parents were in Eden, but God's plan extended to the future with His design for marriage.

So here Adam and Eve both were naked, as man and wife, and were not ashamed. But they weren't alone in the garden. Satan tried to be sneaky and disguise himself as a cunning creature and approach Eve. The scripture doesn't say why the serpent approached Eve. This sneaky serpent tried first to confuse Eve by mocking what God had really said about the trees in the garden. The serpent questions Eve, "Are you sure God told you that you shall not eat of every tree of the garden?" Eve clarifies that they can eat, just not from the tree in the middle of the garden, or they will die.

The serpent convinces Eve that surely God didn't say that they would die. He just doesn't want them to be like Him and know all the good and evil there is to know. So, what does Eve do as she sees this tasty fruit dangling before her very eyes? I am sure her mouth was watering. She picked the fruit from the tree, took a bite, and handed it off to her husband to eat also.

Not only did they immediately have their eyes opened to what had just happened, but they also knew they were naked and felt guilt and shame. They had chosen their own way, rather than following God's plan for them. And it had led them to this place. Ultimately every temptation, no matter how big or small, is to go our own way instead of God's way for our lives. We have a choice.

As soon as we act on the temptations, it's too late. Just like I had hidden the gum I had stolen, Adam and Eve tried to hide what they had done. They no longer stood in innocence. They were ashamed and naked and wanted to hide. God came searching for them and wanted to know what in the world they were doing. They were afraid because they were naked. But more importantly, they were afraid because they knew that they had gone against God. They had no real answers when God started asking questions. All they could do was cover themselves and make excuses.

The results of sin always take us farther than we ever want to go. We experience evil. We have shame and guilt about what we have done, even if we try to hide or stuff it down. We search for coverings. Maybe it's through more destructive lifestyles and unnecessary anxiety. We have a desire to conceal it. We try to put on a happy face and smile as if nothing has ever happened. But what really happens in the process is that we learn to fear God's presence, much as Adam and Even feared

God when He came looking for them in the Garden. We lose that fellowship that He deserves to have with us. We refuse to take responsibility and shift blame from ourselves to anything and everything we can.

What Adam and Eve did was distort God's perfect plan. We see this reflected in the world around us. John 8:34 (NKJV) says Jesus answered them, "Most assuredly, I say to you that whoever sins is a slave to sin." We do not have to be slaves to sin. Adam and Eve sinned, but God came to them in Genesis 3:8 with the promise of freedom from the curse. The Truth that is Christ can make us free if we will choose to become "slaves to God" or, as Paul would say, a bondservant to Christ. Once

you choose to commit to Christ, you will find
untold freedom.

Maybe you've had a past abortion, or
made some other bad decision—whatever it
might be—and you have sinned outside of
God's design. You may have this
overwhelming sense of shame and worries
about what others would say if they found out.
You are struggling. You know it was wrong,
and you cannot get over the pain and regret of
the decisions you have made. Let me tell you:
There is hope.

Do you know what is beautiful about
freedom? In freedom, there is no more
bondage. Romans 10 tells us that if we confess
our sins with our mouths and believe in our

hearts that God raised the Lord Jesus from the dead, we will be saved.

Do you remember a time that you asked the Lord to forgive you? Or maybe you messed up and you keep on messing up. Or maybe you have never asked God to make all things new and forgive you and your past and you are ready to ask Jesus to save you, forgive you of your sins and be Lord of your life. We all mess up. We are human and not perfect. The Bible tells us in Romans that we have *all* sinned and fallen short of what God expects of us. But Romans 10:11 (NKJV) says, "Whoever believes on Him will NOT be put to shame."

All who believe can make the ultimate sacrifice to God, which is to do His will for your heart and soul. Romans 12:1 says that we are to live our lives as holy or set apart to God and that we are to please Him. We should desire to express complete devotion to Him. Don't be molded by the pressures of this broken sinful world. Let's experience a transformation by the power of the Holy Spirit.

The world hates everything about God. That is why it is so important to renew your mind by staying in the Bible and taking time to listen to what the Holy Spirit is speaking to you in that small still voice. Take the time to journal while listening to praise and worship music. Talk with trusted spiritual leaders. Then serve God with the spiritual gifts He has given you.

I know. I know. You are probably saying, "I don't have any gifts." It took me a while before I realized that I had any gifts at all, let alone gifts that I wanted to be used by God. He has equipped all of us for service. If you have trusted Jesus and called upon Him to save you, you have a special call for ministry and service. No matter what you've done or been through, He has big plans to point others back to Himself through your story.

Sometimes we just listen to the wrong voice way too long. I know I did. Maybe we all just need some good southern comfort food and a whole lot of Jesus.

Biscuit, Gravy, and Jesus

Church on Sundays was very much a tradition in our family. Our whole family attended Smoky View, a little country church on the hill off the main highway. Smoky View has the most breathtaking view of the Great Smoky Mountains National Park. It is beautiful. My cousin's husband was the pastor growing up, and our church was a true lighthouse on the hill in our community. It still is today. Every Sunday, we made plans to have our weekly trip to Hardee's for some good 'ole biscuits and gravy. You could always count on Granny and Papaw to be at Hardee's saving us a seat—the same spot each week, right smack dab in the middle of the restaurant. Hardee's was fine dining for us—a quick-service breakfast meal. We loved this special time each Sunday morning to let Granny see us in our Sunday best. She would always tell my sister and me how pretty we were in our dresses.

Hardee's breakfast was okay, but you have not had true breakfast until you have tasted my Papaw's homemade gravy and Granny's homemade biscuits. I have met some people who have never had true homemade gravy. WHAT? If you lived close, I would love to whip up some homemade breakfast for dinner and get to know you a little bit more.

You have not lived until you have had some old-fashioned southern cooking. Our family always held food and Jesus in high priority. You can bet that if we were coming to or leaving the church food would be involved. There was something about gathering around the table that would spark conversations about life, whether that be at Hardees or Granny and Papaw's house. These are precious memories that I will always treasure. That's why Sundays were my favorite day. I got to learn about Jesus and eat some good 'ole biscuits and gravy.

It was at this country church where a small "seed" of purpose was planted in my heart in one of the Wednesday night programs they offered. I will never forget that feeling. Do you have a memory from childhood that you look back on? What was it? Maybe it was something that made a profound difference in your life that you still carry with you today. Or maybe your childhood had some painful memories, tests, or trials. Rest in this—your test can be a testimony, your pain can be your purpose, your trials can be your triumph, and your mess can be a message of hope to point others to Jesus.

Romans 12:1-2 (NIV) says,

Therefore, I urge you, brothers and sisters, in view of God's mercy, to offer your bodies as a living sacrifice, holy and pleasing to God—this is your true and proper worship. Do not conform to the pattern of this world, but be transformed by the renewing of your mind. Then you will be able to test and approve what God's will is—his good, pleasing, and perfect will.

These few verses talk about a committed lifestyle. God's people should, in gratitude, offer a dedicated life to Him. Our life should be one that is set apart from the things of this world. We should not be tempted, molded, or shaped by what the world tells us. We should be encouraged to live a life of transformation. A new way of thinking is made possible by the mighty power of the Holy Spirit. What does a transformed life even look like today? How can we step out of what this world demands of us and live sold out to God? For me, it started with a call and a planted "seed" of purpose, but soon I made a turn towards the world that led

me on a path to destruction.

Planted Seed of Purpose

When I was young, our church had a group called GAs (Girls in Action) on Wednesday nights. In GAs, we learned about missionaries all over the world. Occasionally, missionaries would come before our church and share in person. Taking the word of Jesus to an unknown place was always amazing to me. These people traveled to faraway places on that big, huge globe to an unknown land. My 8-year-old heart began to pump very fast every time anyone at our church would talk about missionaries or they could come in person to share themselves. I could picture myself in an unknown place, sharing the amazing story of Jesus.

Right then, at that moment, a "seed" was planted in my heart. I had big dreams as an 8-year-old girl to accept that same call as a missionary. I mean at eight years old, where could I go? Not too far without a driver's license or sense of direction. At 40, I still don't have that sense of direction even with a GPS. I had people tell me as a young girl that being a missionary wasn't reality, so that dream was like a seed embedded within my heart. It was planted, but not given water—not tended or encouraged.

For plants to thrive and grow, they need air, water, nutrients, and sunlight, but without that, they lay dormant. What is cool about the process of dormant seeds is that many species of plants have seeds that delay germination for many months or years, and some seeds can remain in the soil seed bank for more than 50 years before germination. Some seeds have a very long viability period, and the oldest documented germinating seed was nearly 2000 years old based on radiocarbon dating.

I had this "seed" planted in my heart, but it wasn't in the right environment to grow or thrive. This dream of being a missionary would lay dormant like a seed. This situation isn't uncommon. Often the very people we love and look up to hinder us from stepping out in faith from what God is calling us to. Maybe you always felt called to something greater but think it's not possible behind the walls in which you live.

Jeremiah 1:4- 5 (NKJV) says, "Then the word of the Lord came to me, saying: Before I formed you in the womb, I knew you; Before you were born, I sanctified you; I ordained you a prophet to the nations." God knows. He loves us so much and knows our plans for our future. He is waiting for us to trust Him with our whole heart fully. Sometimes it is hard to let go of things we love in this world, but the Lord has so much in store for us.

"Formed," "knew," "sanctified," and "ordained" illustrate the extent to which God was active in Jeremiah's life preparing him for ministry that would involve every part of him. "Formed" revealed that God is the ultimate life-giving source, and is involved with the birth process. Even before Jeremiah's formation in the womb, God "knew" him, implying an active foreknowledge grounded in God's sovereign purposes. "Sanctified" means set apart for God's special use. You are made for a purpose and you were known before you were born. Let that sink in for a minute. You can even fill in the blank. God is saying, "Before I formed you, (insert your name here) in your mother's womb, I knew you."

The day you were born was the day that our Creator knew that the world needed you to fulfill His purposes. He wanted (insert your name here) to go and make disciples. But here we sit like that dormant seed pushed to the wayside. Maybe you have been told you are crazy for even mentioning your dream, or maybe you are afraid of what people will think.

I challenge you to go back to those childhood thoughts of what made your heart flutter and skip a beat. I chose to let that seed of being a missionary die—or so I thought. I didn't think about it again and, for a while, life just went on.

Life Goes On

Life went back to normal eight-year-old things like riding my bike, playing with neighbor friends or watching television after eating dinner at home. Growing up in our little yellow house, we had a fireplace surrounded by beautiful white bookshelves. I remember finding my baby book, sitting down on our green carpet, and holding that pink baby book in my lap. "I'm a Girl" it read on the front cover. (To this day, the protective plastic is on that baby book!)

As I flipped through the pages, I admired my mom's handwriting and how she documented the gifts from those friends who had gifted her this book to journal the start of my life: *My name is Valerie Reagan, born in Tennessee. I belong to my mom, Joy Reagan, and my dad….* My dad? The name in the book was not the name of the man who had been in my home for the last eight—almost nine— years, the man I called Dad. What in the world? I was afraid to ask mom and it took me a while to muster the courage to point out the error in my baby book. How could I bring this up to mom? Could it be a mistake? What on earth would she say? Would she be mad at me? I had to know.

When I finally mustered up the courage to ask, my mom sat me down and explained it the best way she knew how. "Your biological dad left when I was pregnant with you. He had someone else pregnant and married her." She went on to tell me how much Dad loved me and had adopted me as his own when they got married. But "your biological dad left..." were the only words I heard. I was focused on the negative impact that this name, inked in my baby book, had left on me.

I was trying to wrap my mind around those words. It just wasn't connecting in my brain how someone could do this. That was the day that I began to believe that I wasn't good enough. I felt abandoned. I felt alone in our little yellow house. My dad didn't want me. Like the sneaky serpent in the Garden of Eden, the voice of the enemy whispered lies to me, convincing me that what I was hearing was the truth. It was like a song stuck on repeat that I couldn't turn off: *You've been abandoned. You are all alone. Your biological dad didn't want you. He left you.* This news became the measuring stick for my life. Those lies that I believed became the excuse for everything that I would fail at over the years. With every failure, I added to the deep hole of hurt and misunderstanding.

This isn't to say I was living in a horrible home. I wasn't. The dad that lived in my home since I can remember loved me and adopted me as his own. That very act was and is an act of brave, selfless love. He loved my mom and me as a beautiful package deal. When my dad married my mom, he got me, too. He even

gave me a ring to celebrate the occasion. But

even his love for me couldn't take away the

knowledge of what my birth father had done.

After I discovered my biological dad, I

wondered what he looked like or how things

would have been different if he had stayed in

our lives. My granny and mom did show me

pictures of him. It was usually an old

newspaper clipping or a school yearbook. My

granny would always say, "If you ever want to

meet him, I can make it happen." I remember

thinking *What would be the point when all I*

would ask is why? Why did you leave? I

couldn't bear the thought of the things I would

hear. But I was curious about the brother I had

out there somewhere and thought that maybe I

would meet him one day. As curious as I was, I couldn't shake what I now knew. That one revelation—that my birth father had abandoned me—effectively changed my life.

The devil is very tricky. He planted a lie in my mind, and it grew to be so much bigger. If the enemy can grab a small little lie, he can twist and mold it into something so big that it will soon become a massive stronghold in your life. My brain was fixated on the fact that my real dad had left me.

Have you ever played the game "telephone"? You sit in this circle and whisper something in the next person's ear, and by the time it makes it all the way around this circle, you have this big, outlandish story. Many times, it doesn't even match up to what you said to begin with. This is what happens when we believe a lie about ourselves. It gets bigger and bigger and before we know it, we have this big story about how horrible we are. This is the way I felt as years went by.

I didn't talk about my feelings to my parents. I didn't know to ask God to be the loudest voice in my head and break the chains of lies that I had already allowed the devil to forge. This lie that I wasn't wanted, that I wasn't loved, that I wasn't good enough consumed me until, eventually, it controlled me.

Life went on. We vacationed each summer at different cool places. We went to the beach and even Disney World, which was my favorite. I loved riding the rides that I was tall enough to ride. It reminded me of riding my bike back home—hands in the air, so fun and carefree. Ultimately, it didn't really matter what Mom and Dad tried to do to make it better. I truly believed that I wasn't good enough and any small thing that would happen out of kilter would add to the heavy weight I was already carrying around.

I learned to listen to this loud voice of doubt and allow those lies to become firmly planted strongholds in my life. It seemed like the odds were stacked against me. When I was in the third grade my teacher told my parents at a parent-teacher conference that I wouldn't amount to much. How in the world does someone say that!? I did like to talk and socialize a lot more than listen to the work at hand. Maybe that was what she meant, but her words were powerful—as all words can be—and it was those words of rejection and disappointment that drowned any part of my soul that was still alive. That hole of abandonment in my heart just continued to grow. Imagine carrying around a suitcase and putting a brick inside every time you failed or believed something horrible about yourself? My "suitcase" had started to fill with so many bricks that I could build a small outhouse. It was exhausting, and I felt worthless.

I don't know what has happened in your life or what you are walking through right now, but I want to help you to stop believing those lies. Don't let the devil play tug of war with your heart and mind anymore. It is time to give the cutters to the Lord and allow Him to cut the heavy chains off you. You can finally be free of the lies that have been weighing you down. Leave that "suitcase" full of heavy "bricks" at the door and walk through a new one. I can tell you that God has a purpose for all the deep places of pain you've been. He wants to take the pain and use it for His glory and His purposes. It is a daily decision to tell ourselves that God can take those deep places of pain and use them for his greater good. As we begin to tell ourselves what is true it starts to become a daily discipline in our lives that transforms us and those around us.

Today can be the day. You have a big choice to make. You can sit and sulk in the pain of your past or what is going on right now, or you can call on the mighty name of the Lord Jesus. The time to surrender to His amazing will for your life is now. Psalm 46:1-3 assures us that God is our refuge in troublesome times. He is our refuge and our strength, a very present help in trouble. Let us soak up what this means.

Whatever you've been dealing with, whatever hurt or pain that you have weighing you down, can I ask you to trust Jesus and lay it all down at His feet. It may take asking God to take this from you every single day as you learn to depend on Him and Him alone, as you learn to be still and know that He is God and all the goodness He has for you. As Psalm 46:1 points out, God is our refuge, but He so much more than that...

God is our shelter,

God is our protector,

God is our safety,

God is our security,

God is our sanctuary,

God is our safe haven,

God is our safe house,

God is our hiding place,

God is our retreat.

If you must, write this down and tape it to your mirror as a daily reminder. One thing we need to remember here—and this may sound contrary to what we just read—is that *we* are not enough. You are probably thinking *How can I say that I am not enough when we just walked through the fact that God is our refuge.* Stay with me here. *We* are not enough because *God* is enough. If we alone were enough, then what would we need our Heavenly Father for? We can let God into our weakest moments and those pain points of our lives to be our *enough.* He is our strength. He is the great I AM.

The Many Moves

We said goodbye to our little yellow house when I finished my 5th-grade year at our local school district. It wasn't a happy ending. I was saying goodbye to the only friends and school I had known for five whole years. I practically lived at my friend's house and she at mine. We even went to the same daycare after school. She always had fun football parties. That was soon going away. My parents were building a house, so we moved in with my nana.

It wasn't the best time, but we made the most of it. I wasn't in my normal space, and I was now sharing a room with my sister. That is always guaranteed to make arguments abound. We didn't have our own space. Dad was always gone working at the new house while mom worked late at her job.

Starting a new school was hard. Here were these people that had gone to school together for five years. Everyone knew everyone, and then come these strangers who invade your space for sixth, seventh, and eighth grade. It was hard to make friends at first, but it turned out to be the school I remember the most. I wish we could go back to that time at Fairview. Those are the years that I would call the years of many failures. I acted out and wasn't my true self like I was at church on Sundays or Wednesdays.

We were going through many changes at church, too. Our youth group was dwindling to just me and a bunch of boys. I felt like I needed to be some kind of hardcore mean girl. I tried out for cheerleading and boy, was that a disaster. I thought, *How hard it can be to kick your leg in the air?* But apparently, you need to be a gymnast in the womb or something to be a cheerleader. When it was my turn, I remember running to try out with every intention of giving one of those leg kicks that went straight up in the air so elegantly. Yeah...no. It was more like a sad attempt to play the air guitar. I don't know how those older cheerleaders who were judging kept a straight face. I gave it my all. Needless to say, I didn't make the cheerleading squad. I then tried out for basketball, but all I did was run, and I wasn't even really good at that. I did eventually find softball. After all, that is one sport I loved to play, and it turned out I was pretty good at it too.

I also found a way to involved with church. I loved leading GA's. I think it brought me back to the dreams I had as an eight-year-old of being a missionary. I still loved reading about the missionaries, and I enjoyed sharing about the different work around the globe with the girls that attended GA's.

But, in the quietness of my own room, I had started to despise myself. It seemed to be where those lies of how bad I was or how no one cared about me became the loudest. I listened, and, at the same time, wished it would all go away. I found that giving in to the pain I was already drowning in did took my mind off the thoughts that echoed in my brain. I would cut my leg at my ankle. I didn't want anyone to know, so anytime I was upset, I hurt myself more. Even in a house filled with love, I was so lonely. I didn't really understand that God was with me, even then. I am not sure what place of pain you are walking through, but know you are not alone.

David understood pain, too. He wrote about it numerous times in Psalms. In Psalm 12 David cries for help and for salvation and deliverance. David knew that his only help would come from God. God responds to the cries of His people and reassures us of His presence. We may be in different types of brokenness in our lives. A broken heart is a result of someone's actions whether intentional or unintentional. The broken heart you may have can be the result of rejection, abandonment, oppression, abuse, or even the death of a loved one. You can feel very shattered, like a piece of glass shattered on the floor. There are so many broken pieces, and you have no idea how it may be made whole again.

I have good news for you. God wants to deliver you. Psalm 34:17-18 (NKJV) says, "The righteous cry out, and the Lord hears and delivers them out of all their troubles. The Lord is near to those who have a broken heart, and saves such as have a contrite spirit." Jesus addressed the underlying nature of a broken heart on several occasions. He dealt with fear in Mark 5:36, rejection and feelings of isolation in John 14:16, and despair and loss of will in John 14:1. Jesus understood it all. As a man on this Earth, He experienced the worst of life.

Reach out to the one who can heal your broken heart: Jesus Christ. He loves you and will do extraordinary things to find you in your brokenness. The song, "Reckless Love" by Corey Asbury says it perfectly as I share it in my own words:

There is no shadow that the Lord won't bring to light,

There is no mountain too tall for him to climb up and reach you.

He will tear down was is enclosing in on you and shred every lie, coming to rescue you.[2]

He is waiting for you to reach out. Dive into His word, find the strength to reach out to a professional counselor and trust that God has something new for you. I didn't know this. So, here I sat like an open wound; I wouldn't allow the true ointment to be soaked in to bring healing and hope in my life. Isaiah 53:5 says that we are healed by His wounds. He died so that we could have complete healing. He wants to bring everlasting healing to your life. Are you ready to open up the wounds you've been

---

[2] "Cory Asbury – Reckless Love," Genius, October 27, 2017, https://genius.com/Cory-asbury-reckless-love-lyrics.

hiding under your sleeves and let Jesus make it right? If you don't, that pain will follow you.

I didn't make my life right with the Lord just yet and allowed the pain to follow me to our next new house. This new house was just a subdivision over, so luckily, I didn't have to change schools. Our new house was pretty much the same, a little bit bigger, but just in a new location. Instead of a two-car garage we now had a three-car garage. Nothing changed for me moving into this new house, I was still the same person. My wounds of abandonment and brokenness still followed me. The room I sat and sulked in would soon be a thing of the past. Now, I would have a new room to carry these negative voices too. This would be the house where my life would change forever.

The New House

The funny thing about moving is that it really isn't new. It is in a sense, but you are still bringing your old stuff with you. You don't get brand new furniture, appliances, bedding, and décor every time you move. The same is true with emotional baggage. The hurt and pain still followed me, like a suitcase overflowing with heavy bricks.

Now, it wasn't doom and gloom all the time. With this new home came some cool new adventures. We got to fly in an airplane for the first time. We flew to Las Vegas at night and seeing all the lights in the dark was beautiful. The flickers of light all across the skyline of that airplane window was like nothing I have ever seen before. Being Disney crazy like we were, we went to see the original Disneyland and other surrounding places like the Grand Canyon. I wasn't sixteen yet but had my learner's permit and got to drive on Route 44. That was the coolest thing for me—driving on a road in the desert and everything around you was so flat you could see nothing but road for miles and miles. It didn't have the same effect as my bicycle did when I was a kid, but it was still a fun experience. Disneyland wasn't what we thought, as it was much smaller than Disney World. I remember laughing on the bench with Dad, Mom, and my little sister as we waited to load the tram to our car. A family beside us was sharing how they had five more days at the park, and we looked at one another and thought, *Man, we saw it in one day!* We were a family on a mission when it came to an amusement park.

Now that we were older, we had the opportunity to stay at home by ourselves. That meant that as soon as vacation was over, it was time to spend our weekdays doing household chores and cooking dinner before Mom and Dad got home. This meant I was the one cooking dinner. Once I tried to cook a turkey. Mom was giving me the play by play on how to cook the turkey, and I'm sure she got a real kick out of my lack of enthusiasm in sticking my hand up inside the turkey. Never again. Never. She probably didn't like to fix turkey either and thought maybe I would. Nope. Never will I subject myself or my children to cooking a turkey ever again. Did I say never? I will be the first to sign up to cook the ham. I will just be the ham girl that always takes a ham to any dinner.

I couldn't wait until I turned sixteen because that meant I could get my own job. That is what I did, too. I took my truck and pulled up at a restaurant that was about to open and was hired on the spot. Waiting tables was pretty easy for me. I loved to talk, but not too much and I kept the customers' drinks full. That was something dad would always complain about when we would go out to eat. The tips were like a cool bonus for doing a good job. In my first two weeks of waiting tables, I was able to buy my class ring. That was such an exciting accomplishment for me. I had my own money and that meant I could shop for my own clothes too. The restaurant where I worked was a little bit southern, I mean we are in Tennessee, after all. Our work dress code was overalls, and we had these silly buttons that said, "Ask me why I am number two?" If someone did ask, we had buttons in our overalls that we would give out that said, "Because you are number one." I would make a big deal out of those buttons, and the customers seemed to love it.

It took about a month and I was promoted to the lead when I was on shift. I got a dollar raise and was excited that I made $3.13 an hour plus tips. I depended on those tips. I was a very hard worker when it came to my job. I think it helped that I didn't have to be alone in my room and could spend my evenings serving others in whatever job I had at the time.

Dad gave me a red Dodge Dakota truck. It was his and he ended getting a new truck for himself. Having a car meant some new responsibilities. I was responsible for making sure it had gas which I had to pay for and I had to pay for my own car insurance. Having this truck to myself, I was able to drive to and from school. I would always leave early so I could hang out with the other kids at a local gas station before school. Then, I had the great idea to skip school during class time one day. Always remember that when you don't do something the right way, there will be some kind of consequence.

I think my first bad decision was skipping school. I was a Junior in high school and it was a pretty fall day around September or October. Right when the leaves start to change on trees and the temperature is just right—not too cold or hot. It was perfect weather to ride with the windows down and let the warm sun shine on your face and the breeze blow in your hair. My friend and I decided we were going to go to the lake during school, so off we went during class time. (Sorry, Mom and Dad. You are just now finding out about that one!) Driving through the school gate when we weren't supposed to be was so fun. We didn't make it far. You see, having my own car and a new job meant I had to be the one that filled my car with gas, so—you guessed it—we didn't have gas to make it to the lake that day. Instead, we spent our skipped class digging out change between the seats of the truck. Luckily, gas was only 99 cents a gallon back then, or I would have been really in trouble! We got back to the next class without a hitch.

My next adventure in the car was going to the mall. Mom didn't want me to go to any *cool* places in my car. How boring it was to go to school, work, and then home. How would they ever know if my friend, sister, and I made a quick trip to the mall and back? So, off we went to the mall. Now, we didn't make it easy and go to our local mall. It didn't have the "cool" stores. No. We had to go to the mall that was in another county! I remember like it was yesterday. Driving with the windows down, jamming to some 90's rap music louder than we should have, just me, my sister, and my best friend. I noticed a car following us a little close. Then, it was way too close. A sudden stop and that car rammed into our bumper before we realized what had happened.

This was before cell phones, and we didn't know where the nearest payphone was. We were in luck, though, because where we crashed was right next to our cousin's home. The person that hit the truck damaged the whole back end of the truck. Where the guy hit the bumper, it was as if the bumper made a weird "v" shape. The police came to make a report and I shared with the police as I was crying of course that I had family that lived right next to where this car hit us. The truck was still ok to drive, so after the policeman took our information and made sure we were okay, I drove up to my great aunt and uncle's house. I now had to fess up to not only my great aunt and uncle, but I needed to confess to mom and dad that I took my truck somewhere without their permission. This wasn't fun at all. They were glad we were okay, but boy, was I punished. To punish me, my parents made me ride the bus for a few weeks. That really stunk. Not only did I have to confess to my parents, but I faced a lot of questions from friends at school who were wondering why I wasn't driving.

It seemed very easy for me to jump from one bad decision to the next, not processing what I had done or trying to do better. That hole in my heart, that emptiness and loneliness was being filled with worldly pleasures—a lot of them. These decisions became second nature but still left me feeling empty. It was a path that was easy to follow, but it never left me feeling good about myself, no matter how hard I tried.

The four years you are in high school are some of the most important years of your life. Yes, for most students the focus was on sports, what colleges you wanted to attend, and or what type of career you wanted. For me, it was doing what I could do to pass on to the next grade. I had no drive and no sense of direction in terms of what I wanted to do in life.

I always pushed the envelope of disobedience *just* enough, but nothing too drastic. Just enough to make Mom and Dad cringe. We would argue and yell but be okay enough to put on our big fake smiles at church and walk in the door like all was well. Granny could always tell when we were arguing, and I always looked forward to curling up beside her at church. Just sitting next to her, whether she was being silly or calming me down, always made everything better. Especially when she would have us over to make breakfast for dinner or just cook in general. It meant I didn't have to cook dinner before Mom and Dad got home, and we got to spend time with the whole family. Granny, Papaw, my two aunts, and my uncle all under one little crowded roof.

No matter what was happening in life, we could all come together at Granny's table, and everything would disappear for a while. Granny was my hero. She was very much like my other momma. She and Papaw made an incredible team. They had faced some difficulties in their marriage, but they had come through. The doctors had told my Granny and Papaw that my Uncle Benny should not have been born. He was born with spina bifida—where the spine is pretty much on the outside of his body—and water on his brain. The doctors said that Benny wouldn't live through the night, but here he was sitting in his wheelchair at the table, loving every bite of biscuit and gravy-like the rest of us.

Granny and Papaw took care of my Uncle Benny like champs. They worked opposite shifts so they could each take turns caring for him. He couldn't bathe himself or put on clothes, so Granny and Papaw would always take care of that. Benny brought so much life to the family and was the best card player you would ever meet. He was also one serious pen pal. He would write letters to people all over the world. This was before email or the big wave of connecting on the internet. Benny was a true gift, and Granny and Papaw spent their days taking care of his needs before their own.

One thing that Granny taught me the most was that life is valuable. I didn't realize what a significant impact this would have on my life. I knew that when people said Benny's life was not worth living, he very much beat all odds. Benny walked a little bit with the help of walking braces, but surgery had left Benny in worse shape than before. His spine made a clear "s" shape that I could see when Granny was bathing him. She would always say that one day it would collapse, but they made the most out of every day. Benny was very much an inspiration to everyone who knew him.

Many today would say Benny's life wasn't worth living, that he couldn't possibly have an abundant life with the challenges he faced. In this world, we all will have challenges. It isn't up to us to decide which ones we will have. Jesus gives us an invitation to an abundant life. It starts with us responding to

Him in obedience, and then we will enjoy the good life. Sure, it will be hard, but it is in those moments of hardship where we find our true joy in the One who knows our tomorrow. God's ways are higher and better and far outweigh man's ways. When we realize this and choose to walk in this truth every day, it changes the game.

Isaiah 55 invites us to walk in a life of abundance. In verses 10-11(NKJV) it says, "For as the rain comes down, and the snow from heaven, and do not return here, but to water the earth, and make it bring forth a bud, that it may give seed to the sower and bread to the eater, So shall my word be that goes forth from my mouth; it shall not return to Me voice, but it shall accomplish what I please, and it shall prosper in the thing for which I sent it. For you shall go out with joy, and be led out with peace; the mountains and the hills shall break forth into singing before you, and all the trees of the field shall clap their hands." God's word will never fail to accomplish His purpose. God remains faithful in His word. His word restores life to His people as surely as the rain coming down from the heavens brings new life to the earth.

Whatever hardships and surgeries Granny and Papaw had to face with Benny, it was all worth the joy he brought to our family. My sister and I always fought over being able to push him in the mall. He would fuss at us for pushing him too fast in his wheelchair. His life was a gift. Just like your life is a gift, and the lives God blesses you with, whether planned or unplanned. You might be experiencing hardship in your life right now and struggling to make ends meet, but there is always joy and a reason to wake up to another day. Hardships are temporary and will soon pass away.

A Hard Pass

High school graduation finally came. I couldn't believe that I was actually graduating. I had some new friends leading up to graduation that still kept that door of rebellion cracked open for me. I experimented a little bit with drugs my senior year, but not enough to let my parents know, at least not yet. I just knew that my parents would figure out what we were doing, so I didn't ride around with those friends much longer. I always made excuses as to why I couldn't hang out. I laid low after graduation and started going to church with a friend. There, I felt something I hadn't felt in a long time. My heart felt alive, and it felt amazing. The worship filled my heart with so much joy it felt like I was a little girl, riding my bike again—hands up in the air.

This wouldn't last long as the friends I started to hang around with made it very easy to make a hard pass for church to ride around, experimenting with drugs. I made many excuses and believed that if I wanted to stop, I could. But it became much harder every time I was around them. It felt so carefree and innocent. I mean, what could really happen with driving around in your car—until it becomes more. It became so much more that it made it easy to not only leave high school behind but church as well.

Before long, I no longer recognized the person in the mirror. I had slowly drifted down this path of rebellion. I was very much lost and wasn't sure how to find my way back to the life I knew. How did I even get here?

On a Wednesday night, I sat in the back row of our church with my friends. There was one particular girl I had met from another church. We instantly connected; the other one was a friend of hers. So, she always just came along for the ride. At this point, I had been hanging around them for some time—at least a couple of months. We were running around on the weekends partying, drinking, and doing drugs. At first, it was just Friday and Saturday, so I could make it to church and seem like everything was normal. It maybe took a couple of weeks before I was no longer attending church on Sundays or Wednesday nights because we were out partying. I was slowly drifting away from church and didn't even realize it. In my heart, I wanted them to see what I used to see before I started hanging around them and that was the goodness from my church and how I felt when I was there. I was hoping we could change and stop partying, but they seemed to not want to. So, neither could I. I believed that, if I stopped hanging around them, I wouldn't have anyone. I sure didn't want to be alone—again.

One friend leaned over during the service and asked if we were going out afterward. I knew what that meant, and so I smiled and said, "Yes." In my mind, I was saying, *No*, but I felt like I would lose these friends if I said what I really wanted to. Maybe in their minds, they wanted to say, "No," too. I'll never know because I was too concerned about pleasing them. I felt like my worth depended on their friendship.

Oddly enough, that Wednesday night, we were taking communion. They passed cups of grape juice and crackers around and the pastor said that if we had any unconfessed wrongdoing or sin in our life, we were to confess before taking the cup. I could feel that "deer in the headlights" look among all of us on that back row. We whispered to each other that we could not take this. We knew that how we were living at this point was not right—staying out drinking and doing drugs. At this point, I had already crossed the line of having sex outside of marriage. Those things were a stronghold in our lives. It felt as if my choices were now a heavy chain around my neck and added to the long list of heavy burdens, thoughts, and feelings I dragged around for years.

Soon the service was over, and we got in our car, laughter consuming us. That night was the first night I started to feel convicted about the things I was doing in my life. How did I arrive at this point? How could I turn back to where things were? That night I lay in bed and prayed for the first time in a long time. I don't ever remember praying before. Did anyone even hear me? My heart was aching, and I begged the Lord, if He was listening, to help me turn back to Him. I didn't really know what that looked like at this point because I wasn't living for Him at all. I didn't know how I could do it on my own and wanted Him to show me the way. I knew that I couldn't do this by myself.

Not too long after that incident, I was able to share with my friend how I was feeling. How I felt this conviction in my heart of what I was doing was wrong. She shared her heart of not wanting to continue what we were doing either. I was in too deep to stop. I think we didn't know how to stop or just turn away completely. Things didn't change much after that, though, and we continued to run farther away from the church—but not for long. My world would soon change. The Lord heard my cry. Psalm 138 (NKJV) says that He hears us. In verse 3, it says, "In the day when I cried out, you answered me, and made me bold with strength in my soul." He hears our cry!

Do you feel like you have messed up? That your world may be in the midst of chaos right now? Or maybe you have been holding on to things in the past that you have done, and you cannot shake your past decisions. So, you stuff it down and try to forget. Many times, the things we desire to keep hidden are what God wants to use to reach others for Him. Do you desire to be sold out to God's call on your life, but you don't know how or believe he can use you? Maybe you are saying, "You have no idea the things that I have done. God could never use me."

He can. God creates all things. He gives life. He saves souls. He lifts burdens, and He calms waters. When life is overwhelming and it seems like you might sink to the bottom of the ocean, God is with you through it all. He transforms burdens in your life into blessings.

In this moment of my life, I was so weak and wounded; my heart was weary. I had filled every moment with the wrong things in this world. I just wanted to jump off at this point in life and for Him to take this heavy weight from me. Little did I know the journey I was about to embark on would be hard, but that He indeed had heard my cry.

This Cannot Be Happening

Going to work one night I felt weird. It was as if I had butterflies in my stomach. I just stood in the work bathroom and put my hands on my stomach thinking, *What in the world is going on?* Little did I know that *something* was going on; I just had no idea what yet.

That particular weekend was New Year's Eve and all of us rented a hotel for my friend's birthday on New Year's Day. We planned to stay up all night for a New Year's Eve party with friends, but I declined to go out with the crew that night since I had to go in early to work. This wasn't like me. I couldn't shake feeling so exhausted. So, I fell asleep in the hotel room while they spent the night on the town.

I went to work that next week and I couldn't shake this feeling of being so exhausted. I remember describing how I felt that following weekend and my friends asking maybe what if I was pregnant? Why in the world would they think about such nonsense? That was never going to happen to me. Within the hour we were at the store and back with a home pregnancy test. We were all huddled upstairs in her bedroom while we waited for my results from the little plastic stick that was sitting on the back of the toilet in the other room. It was the longest wait of my life. I had visions of happiness flash in my mind of being married with kids, but not now. *This cannot be happening right now. I have plans to have more fun.* I wasn't ready for this test to come back. I went back into the bathroom and I could not believe what I saw: Two lines. Two lines.

My world flashed before my eyes. My friends were trying to be excited while I was trying not to hyperventilate. The room started to spin. *This cannot be true.* I called my boyfriend and told him we needed to talk. Thank goodness he agreed to meet me so late. Ironically, it wasn't really that late for us. Typically, this time would have been spent driving around at night to drink and do drugs.

The next steps were crushing. I had this small vision of hope that he would be excited. This small glimpse of a Cinderella story. Only it was the furthest thing away from a Cinderella story. He was not excited at all. This was a major problem. He told me that we could take care of this. We could just get an abortion, and no one would have to know. We could just get it done and over with. Get "it" done and over with. I was crushed.

That whole evening was pretty much a blur, and it wasn't long before we both were sitting in his family living room for a meeting. Without a word I went, hoping that somehow some way, he would change his mind. His parents seemed supportive, but it all was a fog. I remember him being so upset and running out of the house. The next thing I knew, I was at home curled up in my bed heartbroken.

I called my Aunt, and she encouraged me to tell my mom as soon as possible. I was so afraid. I don't think I truly slept that night, but it was the first time in a long time I had been home. I had been gone for weekends at a time and Mom and Dad had no idea if I was dead or alive. I was mostly just living it up, running from the pain of hurts and not realizing that I was blazing a destructive lifestyle path.

Before this pregnancy ordeal, we were getting bold about buying drugs, walking straight up to this house that had a special window cut out for a special pass-through for the drug deal. Or bypassing the middleman and going straight to the dealer himself. We could have been thrown in jail or worse, I could have been found dead. I didn't think about the repercussions. I had lost touch with reality. Until it slammed right into me. Now I was just worried about telling my parents that I was pregnant.

That morning there was a knock at my bedroom door. I cracked the door open hoping my mom wouldn't see my swollen eyes, bloodshot eyes crying all night. She didn't say a whole lot. She had already guessed the secret that I wasn't ready to tell. She spoke softly through the door and said, "You are pregnant, aren't you?" She knew. I didn't have to answer, and the tears began to puddle in my eyes and slowly fall down my cheek. She said, "Well, is he going to marry you?" That was a hard "no". My mind flashed back to the hard conversations of rejection I had endured not many hours before. Mom told me that I would have to be the one to tell my dad.

Confess to my dad? That was the hardest thing I would have to do. I think it was because I knew I had messed up. I did tell Dad, and he didn't speak to me for three days. That was probably the most difficult thing for me because I knew I had disappointed him. Looking back, I realize that if you don't have anything great to say in the moment, it is wise to take a minute to gather your thoughts. Words have so much power and what you say speaks so much louder than not having anything at all to say in the moment.

You may have gone through this yourself or know someone who is going through it. You may think there is no one that you can help in a situation like this. Pray about this and ask the Lord to lead you to someone who you can offer life-affirming help to or just provide Godly counsel. You will, without a doubt, come across someone who will be walking in this very situation. The most important thing you can do is be there. Be present and connect her with a life-affirming pregnancy resource center if she is dealing with an unintended pregnancy. Sometimes the best thing someone needs is your presence.

You know in life when we mess up, God is there. In Psalm 103:6-12, we learn that we can praise the Lord for His Mercies. The God we serve is righteous and just. He is merciful and gracious, slow to anger, and abounding in loving kindness. God does not hold a grudge against His people. God does not treat us the way we should be treated. What does He do? He forgives. He is ready to take our mess-ups in life and wipe them away "as far as the east is from the west."

Does that mean we need to keep doing what caused us to get in our mess to start with? No, ask forgiveness and walk the opposite way. Surround yourself with people who can help you walk in His love and mercy. Your local church can help. Get involved in a Sunday School class or small group, seek out your local pregnancy resource center (PRC) and ask if they are hosting any support classes. There is hope and help available. You can search https://www.heartbeatinternational.org/worldwide-directory to find a PRC near you.

All Alone Again

After I told my dad that I was pregnant, he didn't speak to me for three whole days. The silence was so hard for me. I knew that I had disappointed him. When he finally did speak it was as if everything was normal, but deep down I knew I had messed up. My friends were there for a little bit, but it became weird really fast. We didn't talk much about the night I found out I was pregnant when I was with them. Something had clearly changed, and it wasn't them—it was me. We were going out on the town like we always did, but it was awkward. I was always starving and had traded my baggie of drugs for fruit to feed a hungry human growing inside of me.

We called the night early, but I knew exactly what they were going to do. It was what we had lived for the past eight months. They were moving on without me. This was exactly what I had prayed for when I wanted to get out. I didn't realize it at the time, but the Lord had heard my very cry. He knew the plans and path I would take. He knew even when I didn't understand.

It truly hurt. I didn't bring to the table what they were searching for anymore. I was hoping they would still be there, but like me, they were so far into this lifestyle of temporary fulfillment that they didn't see a way out either. I came back home alone, and it was painful. I was by myself and felt like I had no one. I now had eight months before my baby would make her arrival. I dealt with a lot of morning sickness. There was something about the smell of the store which never bothered me before, now became so overwhelming. The smell of the store would hit me as soon as I would walk in and I started every day for the next several weeks like this—getting sick in the bathroom before I could even clock in for work.

So, I dove into my job and focused on doing what I could do to go above and beyond my normal duties. It always came natural to me. It was around April that I got promoted to manager, which was helpful. The promotion allowed me to work the day shift. My mom worked days, too, so this gave us a chance to carpool. It was mostly because I was afraid that I would go into labor on my drive to work, so I felt safe having her with me. Being promoted to manager allowed me to pour my heart into work and making my department the best. It helped me not think. God was truly working in this place and behind the scenes. He was moving in my midst just like He does with all of us.

It reminds me of the song, "Waymaker."[3] The one I normally listen to is by Michael W. Smith. Take a moment as I share in my own words, or better yet pull it up on YouTube and sit in the stillness of the goodness of God.

---

[3] "Michael W. Smith (Ft. Madelyn Berry & Vanessa Campagna) – Waymaker (Live)," Genius, February 1, 2019, https://genius.com/Michael-w-smith-waymaker-live-lyrics.

The song talks about God moving in our midst and wherever we are we can worship Him in that moment wherever it is. God does make a way, He is making miracles, He keeps His promises, and He is our light in the darkness. He is in our midst.

Little did I know how much the Lord was working behind the scenes. He is working even when we can't see or feel it. He will never stop working on us. Have you ever felt you were all alone? You aren't. So many people want to be in your corner; you just need to reach out.

At some point in our lives, most of us will be beaten up, battered, bruised, and exhausted by this world and the daily issues of life. We can rest in knowing that God is the

Lord of our life. He is the Great I AM! He is the I AM for every SINGLE need in our life. Here are a few names of God when we feel all alone. He is...

- Our bright morning star...Revelation 22:16 (NKJV), "I, Jesus have sent My angel to testify to you these things in the churches. I am the Root and the Offspring of David, the *Bright and Morning Star*."

- Burden bearer...Psalm 55:22, (NKJV) "Cast your burden on the Lord, and He shall sustain you; He shall never permit the righteous to be moved."

- Comforter who wipes away tears…Revelation 21:4 (NKJV), "And God will wipe away every tear from their eyes; there shall be no more pain, for the former things have passed away."

- Faithful friend…Proverbs 18:24 (NKJV), "A man who has friends must himself be friendly, but there is a friend who sticks closer than a brother."

- Healer…Psalm 103:3 (NKJV)," Who forgives all your iniquities, who heals all of your diseases."

- Redeemer…Psalm 19:14 (NKJV), "Let the words of my mouth and the meditation of my heart be acceptable in Your sight, O Lord, my strength and my Redeemer."

These are just a few of so many. This is just the beginning of who God is. The phrase "I AM" in Hebrew is closely related to God's intimate name, Jehovah or Yahweh as shown in Exodus 6:3, which happens to occur more than 6,000 times in the Old Testament. My challenge to you is to take 15 minutes a day and research those *"I AM"* verses in the Bible. A great place to start would be to look up https://www.blueletterbible.org/ and search for "I AM" and dive into your Bible and ask God to speak to you. Then take 15 more minutes and journal how you feel God is speaking to you.

Do this for a month and see how your perspective will begin to change.

Everyone Needs Fram-i-ly

The first step I took after several home pregnancy tests was to go to the walk-in clinic. I remember my Granny and two aunts went with me. It was so comforting to just be in the arms of my Granny. She helped wash away all the "what ifs" even when I was so scared.

I was about to turn eighteen, so I pretty much had to grow up quickly. The walk-in clinic did confirm that I was pregnant, so my next step was to make an OBGYN appointment. My Granny and aunts took me shopping that day after confirming my pregnancy at the walk-in clinic. It was of course, too early to know what I was having, so we got a book for me to journal about my pregnancy. Spending time with them was just what I needed. They helped me take my mind off the hurt and pain of all the shame and guilt I felt. Being with them made me feel alive, and I dreaded going back home. It wasn't my mom, dad, and sister; they were always great. It was that I had messed up—big time—and I knew I was a disappointment. Those negative voices of all my failures seemed to work overtime when I was alone.

I dreaded going back home because it meant going back to my room. In my room, I felt as if my world was crashing down. I felt all alone again and those feelings and lies I believed about myself were like a fresh wound that wouldn't heal. That hole in my heart that I stuffed with every negative emotion and fault made the baggage I carried even heavier. My mind flashed back to when I opened my baby book for the first time and all those thoughts were coming alive again.

He left.

You are worthless.

No one loves you.

You failed big time.

This time, the heavy load I was carrying became too hard to bear and I cried myself to sleep for the gazillionth time. The guy who wanted me to have an abortion was now having his family say that they were going to take my baby away when I had her. I wasn't even at the halfway point in my pregnancy, and this caused a lot of anxiety and more negative thoughts added to what I was already feeling. I had nightmares that I had given birth and woke up screaming in the night that my baby was gone. I dreaded going to sleep because I knew the pain that these nightmares would bring.

The first few months, it was pretty easy as not many people knew that I was pregnant. But Mom and Dad did eventually share the news with the church, which made me uneasy going there, knowing that they knew that I had messed up. It was hard getting back into the routine of what I had walked away from for eight months. It did feel good to have my family rally around me and some great family friends who I call "framily"—friends that are family. They were, in every sense of the word, the "best-est" friends anyone could ask for. We hung out pretty much every weekend, and it felt good to be near family and framily, who loved me despite my faults.

Everyone needs a framily. To this day, we may not see each other all the time, but when we do, it is like a reunion with my favorite people in the world. They would give you the shirt of their back and be by your side no matter how late you would call in the night. They were the first friends that we told that I was having a girl. We shared everything with them.

A girl that would change my life. A girl that would literally save my life. Don't you love that God has a specific purpose in our pain? Little did I know that this was just the beginning of beauty from ashes. I first had to get through

these hot summer months of being pregnant.

Hot Summer and Cat Vomit

This chapter may not be for my friends with weak stomachs, but it is funny, to say the least, and it once again demonstrates how thankful I am for my sweet Papaw and Granny.

Six months into my pregnancy, we were in the throes of the rising temperatures. I had a small basketball emerging from my mid-section as my sweet girl began to grow and grow. My feet were swelling just as much as my growing belly was. As the hot summer went on, and I could no longer enjoy hot days by the pool without propping up my feet with cold cabbage wrapped around them—that little tip from my doctor was a lifesaver in the summer heat.

It was the middle of summer and the rest of the family was gone on vacation, so I stayed home and had to tend to the things at the house. I was getting to this point in my pregnancy of going to the OBGYN regularly, so I needed to stay home not miss an appointment. I didn't have covered leave at my job, so that meant I needed to save all my days off I could. I wanted to make sure I had plenty of time to spend with my girl after she was born. I wasn't all alone in the house. We have three cats to keep me company. I wasn't really excited that I was going to be alone with the animals.

We always had animals. I can't tell you how many cats we had over the years growing up. Sorry to my cat lovers out there, but I despise them. We didn't have just one. We had three and their names were Jigger, Highway, and Flippy. They all worked together like the Three Stooges. If I come to your house and you have cats, I can tolerate them, but I can't guarantee that I won't have flashbacks of the evil fur trickster trio. I kid you not, they pretty much haunted me during my pregnancy.

I had an OBGYN appointment, and it was the one appointment where they share all "what to do and what not to do" information. After the doctor discovered that we had cats, they told me that I needed to stay away from their litter pan. I took that advice to the extreme, and I believe the cats knew this. I not only stayed away from the litter pan, but I made every effort to stay away from them—

period. They made every effort to rub against my leg oh-so-nonchalantly. My sweet Papaw volunteered to stop by and change the litter pan while Mom, Dad, and my sister were having fun at Disney World.

My Granny shared my same disdain for cats (or maybe I shared hers.) She fed the neighborhood cats who hung around the house, and she could never figure out why they wouldn't leave. This still makes me giggle to this day. Her intentions were sweet, but feeding them didn't make the furry friends run away. They stayed around and she would just keep feeding them.

My days were filled with working, eating, napping, eating, napping, and sleeping. It seemed like I was always eating towards the end of my pregnancy. It was a good thing I finally had an appetite because I had been so sick the first few months of my pregnancy. Growing a human was a little tiring. I would come home from work, nap, eat, and then go to sleep with my pillow collection. I had a pillow under every growing part of my body. The Three Stooges, aka cats, had other plans. At this point in my pregnancy, I was very hormonal. No matter what happened, I would just cry. It could be a Sonic commercial, and I would tear up. I did have a love for their Route 44 cup of crushed ice, especially on these hot summer days.

One particular day, I got home, and the cats were taunting me. Oh buddy, did they ever have a surprise for me. VOMIT. And it was everywhere. It was as if they made a trail for me to find. I stood in our little house and just sobbed. You know, the kind of cry that is uncontrollable and snotty while big tears run down your face.

I was not about to touch it because I was already under the impression that the litter box was going to come alive and strangle me in my sleep. I ran to the phone and called none other than my hero—my Papaw. Granny answered and thought something was wrong with me and the baby. She also had a few choice words about the cats that I won't share. Then she told me to just lay some paper towels over it, and Papaw would come the next day and clean it up. I let out a few last snorting sobs and thanked them so much for Papaw coming to save the day.

I was so ready for Mom and Dad to come home and enjoy these last few months of my pregnancy. Papaw came to my rescue that next day. He always shows up, just like Jesus! My Papaw was my hero for a situation that seemed so silly to some. I realize that many people face all types of situations that we need to be rescued from. It could be anything from career changes, relationship problems, money issues, loss, most of us at some point will face something beyond our control. We will face something that we need to call for someone to help us. Many times, we look for "heroes" to save us from desperate times. Most of the time, like for my Papaw, he did help me when I needed him most.

What we do need is someone who will never fail us and is always there for us. We will never find that in anyone else, but God himself. Sure, someone could be that for a short time, but even then, they would let us down in some form or fashion. God will always be the most dependable person to look to when we need a hero. I was about to see my need for that true hero.

At the Feet of Jesus

Church had become very much like an old faithful friend. I was welcomed back like the prodigal son in the Bible. I had rebelled against everything I knew, but rebellion always has consequences. I had learned that the hard way. I had sought my own desires for so long, but now I was headed in the right direction. What more could I do?

One Wednesday night after church I was so full of conviction and fear. Conviction because I knew what had led to this pregnancy. It was my very rebellion against God, but this sweet girl growing within me was the innocent party. I had fears about being a good mom, and fear from the many nightmares of her being taken away from me. How in the world was I going to raise her and be a good mom? I knew I couldn't do it alone. So, I went back to where I knew I could find the help I needed. Church was already over, but I needed to step in and just go pray at the altar. I felt a longing to just lay everything down at the feet of Jesus. There were many people still talking in the hallway, so I knew I had time to just go into the sanctuary by myself. I opened those sanctuary doors and entered as a broken body that was soon going to be made whole.

The invisible luggage full of heavy bricks—every single hurt, lie, shame, guilt— you name it, followed me. It was a heavy load as I walked into that dark sanctuary lit only by the hallway lights. Staring at those altar steps before me and my eight-month pregnant belly, I collapsed in pain.

Pain from the bad dreams, pain from my real dad leaving, pain from the hurtful words of my third-grade teacher, and I just cried as the chains began to break and fall away. It was as if Jesus took off each one so He could get to me. I knew I couldn't do this by myself, and I cried out to Jesus to save me. At that moment I felt a warm touch on my shoulder.

It startled me, and I looked up, but it was just me and the Holy Spirit. My Comforter, my Redeemer, my Savior. It was as if Jesus had taken all the chains off me, burned the luggage full of past hurts, and scooped me up into His arms. At that moment, I knew everything was going to be okay. I did just as the Bible says in Romans 10:13 (NKJV), "For whoever calls on the name of the Lord shall be saved." I called on His name. I realized that I had messed up and sinned and that I needed Him. It was just like the old song, "I Surrender All." And that is exactly what I did. I surrendered it all to Him right there in that dark sanctuary.

I stayed on those altar steps for a while. You see, surrender is not genuine until it is total. I surrendered all my wrongdoings, but it wasn't total for me in that moment. It was as if I checked off a to-do list and was okay with doing some things that the Lord pressed on my heart, but it had to fit into my schedule. I did accept Jesus Christ as my Lord and Savior, but I was very prideful. Shame on me. I was going to do everything in my power to protect myself and my girl and didn't need anyone's help, not even the Lords. Getting saved at that point in my life was like I let the Lord wipe this clean and now I can do this growing up thing all on my own. I was missing out on the true freedom of letting the Lord lead and guide me. Seeking His wisdom by studying the bible and what truths it had for my life. I was pretty much set on my way or the highway.

After that night, things were somewhat different. Those nightmares that I had had for months about my sweet baby being kidnapped were exchanged for sweet dreams. I would have these dreams of giving birth and the nurses laying her on my chest. As I would look down with complete joy, all I could see was this beautiful bright light on her face. This brought so much peace to my heart.

Tales of the Lying Nurse, or So I Thought

We were now in the home stretch of my pregnancy. When you think of being pregnant for nine whole months, it seems like it will be forever, but here I was about to go to the hospital thinking I was in labor. Turns out, it was just a false alarm. Leaving the hospital, I was so upset. The nurse said I was only two centimeters dilated, and they were going to send me home. The nurse said my stomach would get tight and hard during real labor, and I would have contractions more than I already was. Tight? My stomach was already stretched to capacity with several stretch marks to prove it, and the nurse had the nerve to tell me my stomach was going to get tighter than it already was? The whole family was sure this was it, and we had all caravanned to the hospital only to have the nurse tell me that I couldn't stay. That nurse was definitely telling lies—or so I thought.

"I am not coming back until she is hanging out between my legs!" I declared, waddling out of the labor and delivery unit. Pregnancy was causing me to show my true colors that day. My mom laughed as I blurted out my demands and that made me, extremely pregnant and hormonal, even more upset. We stopped by our local shopping mall to clear my head and walk a bit more and then headed home. I just wanted to take a shower and cool off and get some rest with my 50 pillows tucked under every crevice of my growing body. I did have an eight-pound human that I was toting around, you know. Little did I know, I had a long night in front of me.

In the shower, I felt an odd release in my body. I thought my water had broken as I looked down to see a small clump of gel-like substance. I later learned that this was called a mucus plug. It forms during pregnancy, helping block the cervix. When someone loses this, it usually means that labor will begin soon. Surely, this would mean that it was almost baby time. The beauty of the birth process, God's very handiwork, was upon us. I was trying to hype myself up that this was really *it* this time. It wasn't scary; it was more a relief. It was time, and I was more than ready. Even though I had no idea what having my daughter would look like, I just knew I was finally ready to meet my girl. We had already been through so much together in these short nine months. We began rushing around the house making sure I had every item in my hospital to-go bag for real this time. The whole family piled in the van to make the drive back to the hospital and this time, the nurses agreed to keep me— Hallelujah!

At first, it was exciting to be sitting in a wheelchair headed into my hospital room. My mom and I had taken the birthing classes and felt well-prepared for the night ahead. I was going to try my best to have a natural birth. As it turns out, that didn't happen. (By the way, kudos to my all-natural ladies out there. I applaud you and would love to sit and have a cup of hot tea or coffee with you to give you a high five and hear your story.) My mom and I had sought out the perfect smelling calming lotion to rub on my feet, and we were ready.

My contractions were picking up and yeah buddy, did my nurse get it right. (Sorry to the nurse for the things I said when I was pregnant.) My stomach did get hard and tight. My mom, being the precious mom that she is, got the lotion out to rub on my feet. She began putting the lotion on my feet, and this awful smell filled the hospital room. "What *is* that smell?" I asked mom. My mom told me that it was the lotion, but it didn't smell the same as it did the day that we picked it out. It smelled horrible! My mom quickly wiped all the lotion off my feet. My poor momma! I am so glad she didn't leave me with my mood swings and all. She stayed right by my side the whole time.

My labor was long, but I got to sleep most of the time. After all, I was headed to bed before my sweet girl decided it was time to make her appearance known. The natural birth idea didn't last. My nurse explained that my contractions were going to get more intense, so I ended up having an epidural, but I was in labor for so long that the epidural ended up wearing off. The nurses had me turning all these different ways to try and help my girl arrive on her own. After worries about an emergency C-section, the most beautiful thing happened: my sweet baby girl entered the world. All the past emotions, trials, and heartache stopped for a moment when the nurse laid my baby girl on my chest. All I could do at that moment was cry, cry, and cry some more, and say, "My baby, my baby!" In that moment that she was lying on my chest, the world just stopped, and I knew I would protect her with everything in me. Little did I know that God had way more in store than I ever thought possible.

The Voice of God

Cayleigh was perfect in every way. I couldn't stop staring at her sweet little face. I couldn't believe this moment was even here. I couldn't believe I was holding her, and that I had been given this opportunity to be her mom. It was the greatest honor the Lord had ever given me. I couldn't put her down. I would just hold her and whisper how I would fight for her and for us to have the best life we could. We had so many friends and family come to see us; I didn't realize how many people loved us. They brought sweet gifts, and we had to take a photo with every single person who held her while we were at the hospital.

As sweet as that day was, it didn't mean that the lies, guilt, and shame went away. Even now that I was saved, they would yield their ugly heads—mostly when I was alone. Those lies I had believed for so long were strongholds in my life. It was going to take some time to replace those with the goodness of God and His voice of truth. For almost eight months I had had these nightmares. Before that, I had had years of negative self-talk and listening to the wrong voice. I recognized this voice of shame. I was having these mixed emotions after I got saved. Things weren't better. One evening, I was on my way home with Cayleigh in the backseat. The voices of shame started, *You are such a bad mom; you cannot even afford to buy diapers. What a failure you are!* I couldn't help but yell out, "JESUS, where are you?"

Even though I had given my life back to Christ and had become a mother to a perfect baby girl, I was still so broken, and the enemy was working overtime. I had my life and my daughter's life in the palm of my steering wheel. The negative thoughts and voices were so overpowering. My grip became tighter on the steering wheel and the thought of a quick jerk and it would be all over. *If you drive your car off this road NO ONE WILL MISS YOU,* said this small lying voice. *Everyone left you, your friends, Cayleigh's dad, you have no one.* I felt like I had nowhere to turn. Could I be the only one going through this? My hands gripped harder on the wheel and I tried to see the road with my tears flowing down my face.

At that moment I heard a very different voice that shook me. *I SEE YOU.* I knew very well that it was the voice of God, the Holy Spirit, my helper. I wanted to die and end all this hurt and pain, but God. My grip on the steering wheel became lighter and I began to weep out loud and realize what I had almost done. I almost caused myself to wreck that would potentially take not only my life but the life of my daughter. The grace of God intervened on my behalf. The mighty voice of God saved my life. Speaking of voices, let this verse sink in from Psalm 116:1-2 (NKJV), "I love the Lord because He has heard my voice and my supplications. Because He has inclined

His ear to me, Therefore I will call upon Him as long as I live." The mighty God hears us and saved my life that day! When we face trials and troubles, He does something beautiful. He was refining me and my life for His purposes. He reached down and drew me out of the pit that I was in and saved me. His powerful voice was the VOICE OF TRUTH and I knew that in that moment. I had been listening to the very voice that kills for far too long.

I want to speak to those who have had some deep, dark moments like this. Maybe you have dealt with things like this that are crippling, so crippling that you need professional help. You don't have to shake this on your own. The Lord has created some incredibly gifted people to help us through trying times in our lives. Your mental health matters. This is all part of being healthy and whole. Focus on the Family is a great place to start. To request a conversation with Focus on the Family's Counseling Department, call **1-855-771-HELP** (4357) on weekdays from 6:00 a.m. to 8:00 p.m. (Mountain Time). The consultation is available at no cost to you due to generous donor support and you will be able to talk with one of their licensed or pastoral counseling specialists.

Don't be ashamed of seeking help. We all need support, and this is just one way we can overcome this together and get the help we need. The devil calls us by our sin, shame, and guilt, but Jesus Christ calls us by our name: His beloved daughter or son.

The Sisterhood of the New Pants

After God intervened in that desperate moment in my car, my life was a bit different. I started to realize that I was indeed being lied to. The negative thoughts and voices were not words of truth. Knowing that God sees me and knows me and calls us His beloved things started to shift. I began forming some fruitful disciplines. One was still being active in church, but the other was the music I was listening to. What we listen to and the words that manifest in our mind are powerful, be sure it is the right thing.

It was as if every song would speak to me in some way or another. I began to date and was very picky. I knew what I didn't want for me and my girl, even if it took me a while. We all make bad decisions about the people that we allow into our lives. Some people can be amazing on the exterior but lost in the interior and that is what truly matters. I had met a guy that was so nice to me and was head over heels about Cayleigh. She was a cute baby. We knew each other from work and he was nice to me during my pregnancy. I was drawn to how kind he was, so we had gone on a couple of dates. He even came to the house for family dinners. That is when he revealed an interior side of himself that I wasn't aware of.

He had a kind exterior, but the interior revealed these outbursts of anger when he would come to visit Cayleigh and me. Cayleigh was just a baby, and he would keep his voice down so no one else in my house could hear him say these ugly things to me. Cayleigh was only about three months old at the time. We only dated for a couple of months, and his true self was revealed. It never became violent, but it was very much verbal. It was as if the voices I whispered in my head for those many years were now speaking in the flesh. His outbursts would come out of nowhere and at one point when he was saying how I didn't deserve anyone else and he grabbed my arm in rage. It didn't leave a mark, but it scared me. That was the last time I allowed him to speak down to me. I was brave enough to tell him I never wanted to see him again. Verbal abuse and domestic violence are sometimes silent until it is too late. It is never okay to demean someone, raise a hand to hurt someone. That person needs help and sometimes you don't need to be the one to try and fix them.

Several months had passed and I did befriend our dreamy interim youth pastor. We were just good friends, but I could totally see myself with a guy like him. Being that I wanted to be a missionary and he was on a mission for youth, he caught my eye. Mom and Dad agreed to watch Cayleigh, and he and I went on a date.

It was so much fun! We went to eat Japanese food, the kind where they cook in front of you. I forgot how much I loved yum yum sauce! After we ate, we blasted Christian rap to Wal-Mart as we went to go get food for a youth event. That is where everything exploded—literally.

I don't remember all the yummy food we were buying or what event we were setting up for. I just remember that it was taking a while to buy everything we needed. I remember exactly where we were standing when it hit me. There, in the freezer aisle, where it should be cold, I became very hot, and I started to sweat. *Oh no*, I thought. Then my stomach made a sound that made me desperately start to look for a bathroom.

Very matter-of-factly, I looked up at my date and told him I would be right back. I was getting sick, and I was too embarrassed to tell him.

Oh no, oh no, oh no is all I thought as I finally made it to the bathroom. That was all she wrote. I was a goner. This date was officially over. I called my sister and asked her where she was. She was on her way to Wal-Mart. It was a miracle. I threatened her with her life and asked her to buy me some new pants. I could just hear the "I need an explanation" in her voice on this one. I didn't have time to tell her; all I needed her to do was to bring some new pants to the bathroom as quickly as possible!

At this point, I had no idea how long I had been gone or if I had a ride back home. I cleaned myself up the best I could and vowed

to never eat yum yum sauce again for the rest

of my life. This was one time where I hoped

that a guy didn't notice the outfit I had on. We

did go back to the church to set up most of the

stuff for the youth event the next night. He was

a great friend, but I could sense that the vibe

between us was just friends and nothing more.

It didn't work out with Mr. Youth Guy.

Maybe he knew what had happened with the

sisterhood and the new pants fiasco. Maybe he

wasn't ready for a package deal and that is

okay. Meeting him taught me that was there

were incredible men out there who were

genuinely kind and compassionate on the

outside and just as so on the inside. He was a

great reminder that God had someone out

there that would not only love me but love Cayleigh as his own. I was okay, even if it meant that it was just supposed to be Cayleigh and me.

Mr. Youth Guy did show me that there are some incredible men like my dad who not only took me in and adopted me as his own but loved my mom just as much. I just hadn't found him yet. I knew that a husband would be a precious gift from God, and I would be honored if that was God's intention for me.

Matchmaker

Becoming involved in church activities started to become a normal routine for me again, and it felt really good. Singing in the church choir, even occasionally singing some solos, was nothing out of the ordinary now. We did, however, have some changes at our church. Cayleigh was growing up so fast. We celebrated her first birthday and had a big to-do at the house for it. It was so fun to have everyone together to celebrate this big milestone. It felt good for me too because I was at this healthy place in my life.

We had an interim pastor come in while our church took some time to search for a new pastor. My parents and our family friends become close to him and his wife. I remember that our interim pastor's dad was sick and ended up passing away. My parents, along with some others, went to his house to pay their respects and came back to tell me he had a son.

The interim pastor and his wife had two kids: a son and a daughter. They never came to our church, so it was a surprise that they had kids my age. My mom shared how the pastor's son had an incredible gift of art. He drew the seven dwarfs in his room from the movie *Snow White*. I was intrigued because, as you know, we were a little Disney crazy.

Over the next few Sundays, the son and daughter started to attend church. I especially liked it when I had to sing because I could look out in the crowd and see this tall, bleached-blonde haired guy. Jason was cute, and I was convinced that I was singing to my husband. He, however, never looked my way even though I was staring him down the whole time I was singing.

Yep, I was crushing hard. I think his mom knew this as well. We always went out to eat after church and one time, Jason came too. We connected right off the bat. We chatted the whole time, and I am fairly sure that I did not eat any of my dinner. Cayleigh at this point was about a year and a half old and was pretty smitten with him, too, as she flirted and batted her big blue eyes at him whenever he glanced her way.

That first family dinner out led to more dinner dates with just the three of us. Once we went out for Mexican food when Cayleigh was a little over a year old. She was competing for his attention and dumped an entire basket of tortilla chips over her head. We couldn't help but laugh. Something special was definitely brewing.

We dated for about four months and then Jason and his family left for a vacation. While he was gone on vacation, a guy from my past told this girl all the things she wanted to hear. You would have thought I would have learned. Nope. When Jason came back from his vacation, I broke things off. I know. I wasn't thinking straight. We were apart for two years and it was the longest two years ever. It turned out that the guy from my past just didn't want me with anyone. I always say I had a huge brain fart. Sometimes the grass is not greener on the other side; it is greener where you water it.

Then 9/11 happened, and it shook the world to its core. If you were around for that moment, you'll remember how devastating it was. I was 21 at the time and working for a local doctor's office. Our doctor came up to the front and said, "A plane just flew into the world trade center in New York." At first, we thought he was joking. He wasn't. It rocked our nation to the core. On my drive home from work that night, I could not wait to get home and hug Cayleigh. It was a beautiful sight to see many churches open their doors. They were truly shining their light bright when the world seemed out of control.

Seeing people jump to their death and buildings crumble to the ground made me think a lot about life. It also made me think about Jason and wonder what could have happened if we hadn't split up. Those two years apart, I would see him drive by in town or think of him often and wonder what he was up to. Out of the blue, I decided to reach out to him one day. The worst he could do was not answer and ignore my message. So, I took the plunge and emailed him. Not long after, he answered. We agreed to meet later that evening, just the three of us, and go bowling. That night, it was like we picked up where we had left off. We had so much fun. Our conversation just flowed into the night. Cayleigh was up way past her bedtime, but I was okay with that. That day, I knew that he was most definitely the one. I think he did, too. We spent every moment together. He worked close by, and we would always take our lunch breaks together. We packed a small picnic and we set up in our local park.

My Prince

It wasn't long before my parents were planning our next vacation. We were headed to Disney World and Jason was invited to come along. So that summer, the whole family, and our framily were ready for our Disney trip. His family was going to be at Disney World at the same time, and we were excited to meet up with them.

We had a tradition of eating at Red Lobster for the first, official vacation meal of our Disney trip. During our meal, I could sense that something was wrong. Our friend had received a phone call and by the look on her face, we could see that it was not good news. My mom had turned her phone off and our friend wanted to wait until we all could gather outside the restaurant. We were almost done eating anyway, so we finished up and all huddled around each other for our friend to share that my Uncle Benny had passed away a couple of hours earlier. It was as if the air in the space we huddled in outside was being sucked out.

We had just arrived at Disney and checked into our resort and my mom, dad, and our friends asked that my sister, Jason, and myself watch the kids at the pool for a bit while the rest of the family discussed everything about Benny's death. It was decided that we would travel back home overnight, sleep, attend Benny's funeral and travel back to

Disney after because that is what Benny would have wanted.

During Benny's funeral, it was hard for me to get emotional. He was in a wheelchair for most of his life and towards the end, it became so hard for him. The doctors told my Granny and Papaw that he wouldn't live through the night when he was born. He sure did prove those doctors wrong! God had a purpose for Benny, but it was time for him to come home. I imagined Benny running to Jesus and Jesus welcoming him with open arms. It would be selfish of me to want him back. Benny was saved, so I knew that he was in Heaven. He spent his time here on earth being such a light for others. Just before Benny died, he got his first computer, so he could email his pen pal friends from all over the world.

I knew that Benny would have wanted us to finish our vacation with the whole family, and that's what we did. On Monday, we were back at Disney and going to Magic Kingdom. When we go to Disney, we leave no ride untouched. But that particular day, with the hot summer sun and the extra travel, we were spent. We took time to sit down while waiting to catch up with Jason's family to take pictures.

It was just after the afternoon parade, so we had a clear shot of Cinderella's castle in the background. They wanted just me, Cayleigh, and Jason to stand for a picture. It was our first group photo. *How sweet,* I thought. Jason started asking me to pose for these silly pictures. He wanted Cayleigh and me to turn around and point at the castle. I turned back around at Jason, but he was bent down. I told him to stand up because I didn't want to look silly just pointing at the castle.

I turned around again, and Jason was on one knee with a RING! He told me that he loved me, and he wanted to marry me and adopt Cayleigh as his own. He asked me to marry him. I couldn't believe it. We talked about our future on and off for the ten months we had been together. We had sweet lunch dates at the park and would talk about what kind of house we would have and where we would live. He was 24 and I was 22 at this point, and we knew we wanted to be together forever. All I could say was, "OH MY GOSH!" I eventually said, "Yes" to my prince right in front of Cinderella's castle. That was a day that we will never forget. This was the person I had prayed and hoped for. A man to not only love me but to love Cayleigh as his own.

Stepping Out

We had started the process of Jason adopting Cayleigh a couple of months before our wedding. We knew we wanted to make Cayleigh officially his. A family friend that was a lawyer guided us through the process of Jason legally being able to adopt Cayleigh. I had known at this point through mutual friends that Cayleigh's biological dad was married with kids, but I had no idea if he had been upfront with his new family about everything. I did not want to mess that up if he hadn't. Our lawyer was able to talk with him and handle this without the disruption to his family life. I figured this would be an easy process since he didn't want a relationship with either one of us. We found out on our wedding rehearsal night that we could now go through the next step of her being adopted. He had officially signed away his parental rights and that allowed the lawyer to set up the court date.

Jason and I married on July 10, 2004, and he even gave Cayleigh a precious ring during the wedding. It was such a sweet moment. It was weeks before she started kindergarten when we were able to go before the judge to make Jason her legal dad. It was a short and sweet ceremony. Our family was complete, and I couldn't have been happier.

Before Jason and I got married, we had had a rough two years, but looking back it brought me so close to the Lord. We were just shopping one evening and he couldn't catch his breath. He was completely worn out and I teased him, saying he didn't like shopping at Wal-Mart. Luckily, the doctor I worked for got him into a heart doctor the next day. Jason was diagnosed with dilated nonischemic cardiomyopathy. One side of his heart was barely pumping. They couldn't figure out what caused it other than a virus attacking his heart.

That day changed many of us. We were planning to go to Disney World for our honeymoon so our most important question to the doctor was asking if he could ride roller coasters. She said "yes," so that made his day. We weren't sure if the medication would work, so we were going to make the most of our life regardless. If that meant riding the roller coaster at the place that he proposed, we were going to do it.

He went from a very active young man, playing on two softball teams to not being able to mow the lawn without extreme fatigue. The heart doctor started him on some medication and was hoping he wouldn't fall into heart failure. So, those first couple of years, it was pretty scary. We were barely scraping by, the medical bills were very quick to come in, and we were not sure if we were going to have money for food. The Lord was always faithful and always provided our every need through others. Out of the blue, his mom or others would just bring groceries to our home or invite us over for dinner. Or my granny or mom would cook; it was such a blessing without us even saying a word.

At night, I would lay my hand on Jason's' chest and fall asleep just praying to the Lord to heal Jason. It was the first time in a long time that I remember being very specific and regularly praying to the Lord. It became a habit and the more I prayed, went to church, and listened to praise and worship music, the more the Holy Spirit would speak to me and show me things. Serving at church, helping with activities, and volunteering filled me with so much joy.

It took two years with Jason being on medicine to finally be healed. Praise the Lord! Over those two years, we didn't have to pay for a single dose of medicine through the generous doctor that I worked for at that time. He made sure the pharmaceutical reps had given us the samples we needed to get by, and we did. This is just another reminder of those small blessings from the Lord. Then the Lord blessed us in our 3rd year of marriage with another gift—a baby girl! Makinze is another gift and has such a huge heart for others.

During the many altar calls at church, the Holy Spirit would often speak to me about sharing my story of getting saved and how He spoke to me in that moment in my car when I wanted to die. The Holy Spirit went as far as speaking to me in my sleep through my dreams. I would see a glimpse of me, on a stage, sharing my story. That terrified me.

There was no way that I was going to share my messes with the masses.

Everyone thought Jason was Cayleigh's biological dad because they acted so much alike, and I intended to keep it that way. Why go through all that pain and share my past with anyone? Every time the thought came to my mind or in my dreams of me sharing my testimony, it would get shoved down so far to hopefully not be brought up again. It was a hard no. I liked my comfortable life. Occasionally serving at church, singing in the choir, and doing whatever I wanted. I liked my life this way. I had control and occasionally let God do His thing.

This back and forth with the Lord went on for 10 and a half years. I will say, during those years, I had the clarity of His voice from what I went through with Jason's heart condition. I was able to forgive my biological dad for leaving me even though I didn't understand, but it felt good to lay it all down and give it to Jesus. I was able to forgive Cayleigh's biological dad and pray for him and his family. I couldn't do one thing about what had been done in the past but pray. There is power in prayer.

In the summer of 2012, my mom invited me to tag along to a women's conference. I agreed to go, and little did I know, that the Lord was excited to check this off on His purposes-for-my-life list. A beautiful lady shared her story

182

that day which was very similar to mine. Call me "Miss Hot Mess Express"—I was bawling. She had a beautiful story of getting pregnant and making the brave choice of adoption. She shared how she connected with her daughter many years later and it was as if something was rising in me along with the tears. The Holy Spirit whispered, *I told you that you had a story to share.* I couldn't push this feeling down anymore. I had to talk with someone.

I knew at that moment I had to do something. I stopped at a table out in the foyer that day to hopefully volunteer at a pregnancy center. I had no idea these even existed. I still have the sent email in my inbox, and they never responded. I am so thankful I persisted to find a place where I could help. I pushed this away for too long to give up so easily now. I reached out to the Pregnancy Resource Center in Maryville to see what I could do to help. I worked full-time so it was going to be a little tricky. The director shared with me that I could help our church participate in a baby bottle campaign and share my story. This baby bottle campaign would help people in our church be involved by donating change, cash, or checks to the community-funded ministry.

Our pastor was on board with me sharing my testimony and doing a baby bottle change fundraiser at my church. Now, it was time to share my story. The story that God had wanted me to share for so long. Sharing how God pulled me out of the darkness was so freeing, but what was funny was that I thought that was it. I did what God wanted me to do. I thought, *I shared my story—we are done here.* But…He was definitely not done working on me. Your story—and we all have one—is the key that can unlock someone else's prison. Your story can be the key to help the Lord bind up their wounds once and for all. Don't be afraid to share your story. I encourage you to write about how you came to faith in Jesus. The more you write it down and pray for God to send people your way with whom you can share your story, the freer you will feel. God will put people in your path; you just need to be bold enough to start the conversation.

Leap of Faith

Jason was running a marathon in December, and I thought it would be the perfect Sunday to go visit another church with the girls. It wasn't that we were unhappy with our church. We were feeling like our church wasn't home anymore, and we didn't like this feeling of unrest. We got ready that morning and off we went to visit another church in town. The person who I was planning to meet didn't come, but I did run into someone else. All part of God's perfect plan.

She took me by the arm and ushered me to her Sunday school class. I sat in that Sunday school class and was overwhelmed with how at home I felt. I cannot remember what the lesson was about, but I was so moved by how raw and real the teacher was. I just remember sitting at the back of the room soaking in this incredible moment. I was so thankful I disrupted our routine and obeyed what the Holy Spirit wanted me to do.

The girls seemed to enjoy the visit, too, and I knew what we needed to do. Jason got home from his race, and I shared what we had done that day. I told him how we needed to all visit again as a family. I knew if he felt the way I did in that Sunday school class, that God would be moving us to a new church home. So that next Sunday we planned to all go as a family.

Jason did come with us, and the rest was history. It wasn't long until we went before the church to join. I connected with some incredible friends that are still such a huge part of who I am today. They encouraged me to dream and take leaps of faith. I witnessed so many of my friends reaching their dreams. It inspired me and brought forth that dormant seed that was planted in my heart. It was as if they poured Miracle-Gro on my life and encouraged me to not be afraid of taking a leap of faith in what God had for me.

As we settled into our new church home, the Holy Spirit was working overtime. The pastor, and the whole church for that matter, was passionate about the sanctity of human life. I had never before heard a sermon dedicated to that topic. That's sad to think about. Our pastor boldly shared the biblical truth on our worth and how we are valuable from the moment of conception to natural death. Not only did they talk about the sanctity of life, but they also put loving action to their voice in everything they did.

Our church was in a whole sermon series dedicated to the sanctity of human life and promoting the local Pregnancy Resource Center in Maryville. I was familiar with the particular Pregnancy Resource Center only because of reaching out to them from our last church.

I just had no idea what God was orchestrating behind the scenes. Each Sunday in this particular month seemed to be dedicated to speaking on some topic related to the sanctity of life. The Pastor would preach on abortion, the value of life, and why we should speak up for the innocent children and their brave parents. He would acknowledge those who have had abortions and how Jesus can heal them and make them whole. Then it would come time for the invitation. It felt like I was watching a movie of myself. I would flash back to my 8-month pregnant self, walking down the aisle of our old church, and falling at the altar.

I visualized myself surrendering to the Lord in that intimate moment when He saved me. He wiped all my wrongs and became Lord of my life. This made me a bit of a hot mess, reliving that moment of total surrender. Why on earth was the Lord bringing this to my attention over and over again? After church, the Lord and I would have a few words, "Why do you keep bringing up my past, Lord? Just what do you want me to do with this?"

The Lord wants us in total surrender to Him. He wants us to be obedient to what He has called us to. He has a specific purpose for our lives and knows how free we would be walking in full obedience to Him. The Lord can do *so* much more with our surrender than we can ever to with our control. All we need to do is say, "Yes, here I am. Lord, use me however you want to."

Not too many Sundays after that replay of my "movie," I came into the church, opened our bulletin, and saw the job vacancy for Executive Director at the Pregnancy Resource Center ministry. My heart was being pulled in ways that I never thought possible. Could this be why God uprooted us from our other church? Could this be why the Lord was making me relive my past and reminding me of surrendering to Him when I got saved? I had to find out more about this position.

You would think I would get raving support for wanting to know more about this role, but not so much. My husband was grateful that I had a "safe" job, and my dad couldn't believe that I would even consider leaving a good job for "ministry." I remember telling my dad that this wasn't about getting a job in "ministry;" this was about doing what

God had called me to do. There are a lot of unknowns when taking leaps of faith in the Lord. Something I know they were just trying to protect me from any upset. I knew that if God was bringing us to this that He was going to take care of us. So, I submitted my resume and continued to pray. In January of 2014, I sent this email to our pastor:

I may have an opportunity to work for the pregnancy resource center. For the past 2 years, God has allowed me to share my trials and the power of redemption through Christ in my own life at a couple of churches and bring awareness to this lighthouse in the community for those facing the same. God has been wanting me to do more and little reminders for God speaking through you in service gives me

*peace in knowing that this is a calling more
than "work". I cannot say much because of my
place of employment now.*

*If you could lift me up in prayer for
Monday at 615pm. Thank you very much.*

Love in Christ,
Valerie Millsapps

Within the month, I was saying goodbye
to my job and taking a leap of faith in my new
role as Director of the Pregnancy Resource
Center. The Lord may be prompting you to do
something that is way outside your comfort
zone. It may not be in the pregnancy help
ministry. It could be to go overseas and teach
English and share the gospel, or it could be to

serve the homeless, or it could be to help impact the foster system by adopting. I don't know what the Holy Spirit is whispering to you, but go volunteer where He is tugging you. He will show you and you will know where He wants you. It may not be in full-time ministry; you may want to serve while you still work, and that is okay, too.

I do know He doesn't call us just to pay bills and die. He has so much for us and a desire to go and make disciples. It takes us being uncomfortable and taking a leap of faith to serve where He leads. In Matthew 16:24 (NKJV) it says, "Then Jesus said to His disciples, "If anyone desires to come after Me, let him deny himself, and take up his cross, and follow Me." We just need to say yes even if it scares us.

Following Jesus is very much a commitment. Commitment is a daily decision and Jesus surely wastes no time getting to the heart of commitment. We have a choice every day. Either we decide to be committed to what the Lord has for us or we follow our own wants and desires and deny Him. Commitment demands action and it goes beyond our relationship with our Lord and Savior to all the areas of our lives.

Being committed not only requires discipline, but it builds up our faith and develops our character. Charles Spurgeon says, "If you have never believed in him, may you believe in him at once! Why delay? He can save unto the uttermost, believe in him just now. And if you have believed, keep on believing, and let your believing grow more intense. Think more of Jesus, and love him more, and serve him more, and grow more like him. Peace be unto you for his dear sake!"[4]

When you step out, take up your cross and follow Him, the Lord will reveal just how big a need there is and use you to bring glory to His name. God wants us to do His will. The Bible is clear about us obeying the Lord. Here is some scripture to back that up:

---

[4] "The Private Thoughts and Words of Jesus by C. H. Spurgeon," Blue Letter Bible, accessed December 19, 2020, https://www.blueletterbible.org/Comm/spurgeon_charles/sermons/2212.cfm?a=945024.

- Deuteronomy 4:30 (NKJV), "When you are in distress, and all these things come upon you in the latter days, when you turn to the LORD your God and obey His voice"

- Daniel 7:27 (NKJV), "Then the kingdom and dominion, And the greatness of the kingdoms under the whole heaven, shall be given to the people, the saints of the Most High. His kingdom is an everlasting kingdom, and all dominions shall serve and obey Him."

- Acts 5:29 (NKJV), "But Peter and the *other* apostles answered and said: "We ought to obey God rather than men."

- James 1:22 (NKJV), "But be doers of the word, and not hearers only, deceiving yourselves."

Our obedience isn't a "chore" that we hate doing, like matching socks from the laundry. (I loathe matching socks because half of them disappear). No, our obedience shouldn't be something we loathe, but something we *love*. Serving and wanting to do God's will should be out of our love for Him and what He has done for us. If we love the Lord, we will desire to serve Him in every way possible, and in serving Him we will also want to obey His commandments that He has for us.

If obedience is not something you've always been used to, it is something that is learned. We all have to practice and have a desire to help others learn this skill as well. It is easy to become disobedient. Romans 11:30-32 (NKJV) shares a little bit about that and how we can make a new choice today. It reads, "For as you were once disobedient to God, yet have now obtained mercy through their disobedience, even so, these also have now been disobedient, that through the mercy shown you also may obtain mercy. For God has committed them all to disobedience, that He might have mercy on all." We are human and all fall short. The Lord offers His amazing mercy, mercy that we don't deserve, and his complete and total forgiveness when we

confess that we messed up.

The Need is Great

Stepping in this ministry role was like a toddler stepping into a toy store for the first time—bright-eyed and ready to explore all the things. When God led me to the Pregnancy Resource Center, I knew I was exactly where He wanted me, but what I didn't realize, was the reality of the task was before me.

The burden was heavy. Learning that we had a budget to meet and knowing that I was accountable for getting all this money donated to make sure our staff members were able to provide for their families and that we were able to provide for the things we needed medically to run the entire ministry. It was a lot. I am sure God was like, "Oh, ye of little faith".

The ministry side of things was awesome; it was the funding part that scared me.

The ladies coming to our center were pregnant and happy. On occasion, we would have someone who was unsure of what to do. We didn't see many people each week when I started, maybe about 5-8 people a week. Some days we wouldn't see anyone. Even if one person showed, then we were there at that moment in time for that one person. I used to think that abortion wasn't really that common in our area. Boy, was I sadly mistaken.

The beginning of that first year involved learning many of the ins and outs of the pregnancy help ministry. Daily, I remember praying to God, "Okay, you've placed me where you want me now tell me what to do." As soon as I started, I had to start planning for the annual fundraiser. I had dreams that no one would show up, partly because of many hurts still lingering because of my past. People did show up, and it was incredible. That first year we probably saw close to 500 people. Then everything started to slowly change.

In my second year, I started my journey of learning, which I continue to do. I started to slowly make some changes in the ministry. We were still advertising in the phone book! I shifted to online outreach that year and we started to slowly see more people come in. We made some other changes as well. The director before me told me about a pro-life figure that I needed to be aware of—Abby Johnson.

Abby worked for the abortion industry and had to assist in an ultrasound-guided abortion and was completely broken by what she saw. A baby fighting in the womb while the abortionist took the life of a human being before her very eyes. She left the abortion industry and now is an advocate for life and those still working in the abortion industry. I read her book about her journey called *Unplanned*.

This book broke me. One part that stood out to me was the people praying outside the abortion business where Abby had worked. She mentioned some mean people outside the business but was thankful for the faithful, compassionate few that ultimately helped her leave the business. It was ultimately God who met her inside that abortion business and radically changed her life. Those faithful few just followed up on their promises to help.

During my reading about those faithful compassionate few outside the abortion business the Holy Spirit very clearly spoke to me. *You need to go.* What on earth was I hearing? The Lord prompting and wanting me to go outside our local abortion business. As you can imagine, I had a little argument with the Lord. I am not so sure I want to do that but was quickly reminded of my spiritual journey in obedience. Yes, Lord, I will do as you ask.

So, before I went, I needed to call the abortion business. Being very naive about my role in this spiritual war between life and death, I had no idea what God was about to reveal on this journey of obedience.

I called to ask where someone would need to park if they were going to get an abortion. The chipper friendly voice on the other end told me where I needed to go and told me not to worry about my abortion (she assumed I was getting one), that it was very safe. They do five on a slow day and TWENTY-FIVE on a busy day! She also warned me to not be alarmed by the protesters outside, that I could get help getting into the building if needed. She also told me to not take

207

the pink pamphlets that the protesters were trying to hand out.

To say that I was in complete shock was an understatement. She threw around numbers like it was trash. Five on a slow day and twenty-five on a busy day. Each was a living, distinct, whole human being that she was talking about. How could she be so nonchalant about it? My mind was spinning at that point. Protesters? My mind flashed back to the not-so-nice people in Abby's book.

"Lord!", I argued. "I am thinking you're mistaken on this whole standing on the sidewalk thing." I did not want to go, but then I was made aware of a lady that goes faithfully to the sidewalk. I was able to connect with this sweet lady named Esther. If that name wasn't a perfect fit for this day, I don't know what is.

In the Bible, Esther was a woman chosen on the account of her beauty by the Persian King to be his queen. She used her influence to save the Israelites in captivity from persecution. Esther had courage. If anything, this was a sign for sure.

Courage breeds courage. Courage is something we can build. It is very much like a muscle. The more we practice courage the stronger our courage becomes. To every woman reading this, Esther is a reminder of God's power. God used her beauty, her intelligence, and her remarkable, fearless faith to accomplish His will. Through her obedience to the Lord, Esther became a "star" (This is the meaning of her Persian name) in the Kingdom. Esther was a servant and served others.

Esther was used by God to accomplish His purpose. She offered up a moving petition for the lives of her people, swayed a kings' opinion, and was given a specific strategy and resources to save her people.

This same kind of influence is very evident today among women and men all over the world who use their gifts and talents to lead movements, raise up families, and nurture the body of Christ. You, yes, YOU can impact your very societies, in your homes, in your professional sphere, and friends by practicing the same sacrificial attitude of women in the

Bible like Esther. This isn't about whether you have influence or not, it's about whether you choose to use your influence for good or for evil, to increase God's kingdom on the earth, or attempt to destroy it.

I was excited to talk with Esther. Just speaking with her calmed my fears. She had been standing out on the sidewalk on and off for many, many years. That Friday I planned to go and meet her on the sidewalk while still having some hesitation with what the abortion worker confided in me on the phone. As I walked over the hill, there, on the sidewalk stood five feet, two inches of courage and grace.

She greeted me with such loving kindness and made me feel at ease. That day will be a day I never forget. The face of each abortion worker mimicked a stone. They each wore a semi-frown that seemed to be formed permanently on their face from many years of darkness. My heart broke for them as it did for the very people that drove past us that day in fear of the "protesters." I cannot imagine the words that have been thrown around at them over and over again over the years. They glared at me in such deep pain, and it crushed me. Jesus died for them and oh, how He would love to pull them out of this mess.

Tears welled up in my eyes as most of these girls were driving past Esther and myself and they would not even look at us. One particular girl did make eye contact and I was able to share that there was help for her, that she did not have to do this. Those pink pamphlets that the abortion worker told me to steer clear of was a list of alternatives for hope and help if these ladies wanted to change their minds.

That day on the sidewalk was eye-opening, heart-wrenching, and I was flat out mad. That day was busy. This need was so great. Why were these girls coming here? They were tearful and held their heads down like a heavy weight as they walked into the abortion business to take the life of their children. A choice that could never be undone.

I felt completely defeated and any part of the energy to carry on my day was sucked out of me. I was mentally and emotionally drained. There is a feeling out there on that sidewalk and it is not a good one. It is almost as if there is a thick wall of fog that is very heavy and dark. You feel it in your spirit. There wasn't any yelling as I envisioned in my mind when I heard "protesters." Only huge hearts that wanted the women to know they did have a different alternative. Why on earth would the Lord send me out here? Why? I was so heartbroken. Then came a tiny whisper from the Holy Spirit that said *This is what breaks My heart*.

I was undone. What could I do? "God, why aren't you sending these ladies to us?" I received a gut-punch of an answer—*You haven't asked me to send them*. Such a simple answer. I haven't prayed. I had no idea this was going on in our backyard, and in astonishing numbers! And so many were silent on the matter. I hadn't asked. Whoa!

Innocent, living, distinct, whole human beings are being aborted at alarming rates, yet life goes on uninterrupted. I had flashbacks of my own journey and the words, "Just get an abortion no one will have to know. We can just get it done and over with."

My faith journey is a continued work in progress, but this defining moment had a huge step in building deeper roots in God's word and His plan for my life. I was ready to rise up as

HIS BELOVED. When He created and thought of me before I was formed in my mother's womb, He had a plan. He has a plan for you too. You are fully known and fully loved. I knew without a doubt that this was the mission field He had for me all along. It just took some bumps along the way to run with reckless abandon to what He has for me. The amazing part is that I get to invite people to join me along the way.

I did start to pray. Our team started to pray. We engaged with others to pray and God started to move in a mighty way. There is something about kneeling before the throne of grace and asking God to intercede in a big way. Matthew 18:20 (NKJV) says "for where two or three are gathered together in My name,

I am there in the midst of them." He is always there. The Lord is inviting you to something bigger than yourself. I encourage you to find out what that is. You will never be the same.

Your Voice is Needed

Throughout the world, over 42 million abortions occur every year.[5] That is roughly 115,000 abortions every single day. Every single day, 115,000 human lives are lost. Let that sink in for a moment! That means 115,000 lives will never meet the face of their moms and dads, grandparents, great-grandparents, and so on. Abortion leaves a path of destruction, lies, and secrets that is ruining lives every single day.

---

[5] Susan A. Cohen, "Facts and Consequences: Legality, Incidence and Safety of Abortion Worldwide," Guttmacher Institute, December 6, 2016, https://www.guttmacher.org/gpr/2009/11/facts-and-consequences-legality-incidence-and-safety-abortion-worldwide.

Even if you have a story like mine, and many of you do, God wants to use you and your story for His glory. People are waiting for you to interrupt their life and to let them know that they are not alone and that they too can rise as His beloved. That through the trials, valleys, and mistakes, that Jesus will not stop pursuing you. Did you know that the same power that raised Jesus from the grave lives in us?

If you are reading this right now and you have chosen abortion, you don't have to walk around with this secret anymore. I have had the opportunity to speak in many places and share my story of what God is doing through our Pregnancy Resource Center. I cannot tell you how many times that I have looked eye to eye with men and women as they shared, many times for the first time, the deepest place of pain they have ever revealed. Tears well up in their eyes and they whisper that they wish they knew our center existed.

Over and over, I have taken those deep secrets of people all across our community, and across the globe and wept with them, prayed with them, pointed them to the One that can take those deep places of pain and make them new. If you don't know where to turn, there is help. All across our great country, centers like the one I have the opportunity to lead have abortion recovery programs to direct men and women through healing.

You can search www.optionline.org and
get connected to a center near you and ask if
they have an abortion recovery program. You
can also reach out to a couple of different
healing groups. One is
https://www.godeeperstill.org/ and the other is
https://www.surrenderingthesecret.com/. I
know both of the incredible women that lead
these organizations. They have amazing
stories of redemption. Either of these recovery
programs will change your life.

Women and men are being manipulated
across our communities. In a survey sponsored
by Care Net, researchers found that 4 in 10
women who have had an abortion were
churchgoers when they ended a pregnancy.
They are sitting in our churches struggling with

what to do. They are searching on their phones and being led to businesses who will stop at nothing to tell lies to these image-bearers of our Creator so they can hand over money to take the very life created by our Heavenly Father. They tell women and men how helpless they are and how this is the best option and how *it is nothing but tissue*. Friend, let me tell you that is a lie from Satan himself.

We have had women who were led to abort their very own babies in the privacy of their own homes by taking a chemical pill to take the life of their child. We have many women who have shared having to experience gruesome images that they will never, never forget. Or they were sent home feeling as if they were dying and when they called for help, they were told not to tell the ER what they had done.

115,000 lives. I pray that we finally come to a place and get on our knees and cry out to the Lord. 115,000 is *not* just a number. I pray that number becomes very human to us and we see how it breaks the very heart of God. I pray we realize that people are walking around us every single day with this pain from their past. If your church is not speaking up and out in favor of the sanctity of life, I pray that you will speak up and ask them to.

If our churches are not speaking up for the very lives created by our Heavenly Father then our tithe needs to go to the abortion clinic themselves. "Well, that is just crazy," you say.

It sure is. I heard a good friend tell a story of a pregnancy center director that befriended his local abortionist. He kept trying to invite him to church. He would always decline until one day the abortionist made an offer. He said, "I tell you what, I will come to your church when your church stops coming to me." This absolutely breaks my heart. I would rather us speak the truth of the word of God in love than for someone to come to us one day asking why we didn't tell them they had a place to go to for help.

How can you use your voice? There are many ways you can use your voice. You can first ask your church to invite your local pregnancy center to come to share about the work of the center. I know from experience that we are not about taking money away from your church. God works on the hearts of His people on how they should be involved. His supply is in abundance. One of my dear friends and mentor, Marc Newman has always said, "it is better to know about your pregnancy resource center and not need them than to need your pregnancy resource center and not know them."

I know that when I die and come face to face with my Heavenly Father, I will be so thankful that I said yes and did all I could for women and men and their preborn children. I can stand on the infallible word of God and know that I spoke up for the least of these. Our women and men in our communities need to know where to turn in a time of crisis. What a blessing to know that we can say we have done all we could for families that face unintended pregnancies, so they can be thriving parents for their babies.

Just this week I have gotten the sweetest messages from brave moms that I and our center have had the opportunity to form relationships with. It doesn't stop with a pregnancy test with us. We see these brave families as part of our own family. One brave mom invited me to her wedding that will take place after Christmas. Another brave mom sent a text on a milestone of reconciling with her mom. Another mom shared the updates about the delivery of their second baby since they have been married. These updates all came in the same week while writing this to you. We get precious updates like this weekly. This is what it is all about impacting the next generation.

We need to use our voice of compassion and truth to save lives. We have been silent for far too long. Your voice is needed and could be the very one that leads them to know about our Heavenly Father. We can be a part of many great missions, but it is great to be a part of something so much bigger and that is the Great Commission.

God has a story within you. Maybe it isn't with the pregnancy help community. Regardless, your voice is needed. In John Maxwell's book, *Intentional Living*, he says it perfectly: "To be significant, all you have to do is make a difference with others wherever you are, with whatever you have, day by day. Some may say that the problems look too big for us to tackle. We say to ourselves, "What can I do? I'm just one person."[6] You were made to live a life of significance.

One person is a start. One person can act and make a change by helping another. One person can inspire a second person to be international, and a third. It is the very root of servanthood. Becoming great in Jesus' way. Even before Jesus went to the cross, He made sure that His disciples understood servanthood. They were able to witness and watch in awe as He redefined leadership by

---

[6] John C. Maxwell, *Intentional Living: Choosing a Life That Matters* (New York: Center Street, 2017).

taking a towel and washing their feet. We are servants making an impact for His Kingdom.

Jesus was the very model for each one of us in serving and sharing. I hope you know just how valuable you are. You can trust God with your past! Every step of obedience is a step back to the Father. We can expect great things from God. We just need to pick up a "towel" and wash others' "feet". Serving others is the very heart of God. People need you. Your Story. Your Voice. Don't wait. If you want to really live a life that matters, don't start when you think you have everything together and right. Just start. If we wait, we will miss the very stories our lives could be.

Do you know what is beautiful? About nine months (October 29, 2014, to be exact) into me serving as the director, I received a reply to a Facebook message. It threw me off guard because I had sent my message on December 27, 2008. I had sent a message to my biological brother. I found him on Facebook and was dying to get to know him. If I were in his shoes, I would want to know that I had a sister out there somewhere. He hadn't responded for six years. The message ended with, "...if you are my sister, I wouldn't want to go another 33 years without knowing you. Anyways, I don't know what to say...tag you are it."

That message resulted in me meeting the whole family, and even though I never knew them, it felt like we never missed a beat.

Meeting my biological dad was awesome.

Walking through the forgiveness process so

many years prior, and praying for my biological

family had indeed prepared me for this moment

of my redemptive story. God was and is with

me and you always, even in those darkest

hours. We can walk in the promises of Christ

Jesus knowing that He can heal our hurts and

through this we find strength in reaching out to

others, trusting that God does have something

for us.

Lamentations 3:22-24 (NKJV) says,"

Through the Lord's mercies we are not

consumed, Because His compassions fail not.

They are new every morning: Great is thy

faithfulness. 'The Lord is my portion,' says my

soul, Therefore I hope in Him!" When you got up out of bed this morning, if you have trusted Jesus as your Lord and Savior; He is always there. Circumstances in life can let us down, as can the ones that love us most, but God is always faithful.

His presence is assured even when you are unaware. What joy it is to know and experience His mercy and faithfulness. People need your voice, but not *just* your voice. They need to hear from those who are rising up as His beloved and allowing the Holy Spirit to speak in and through them. Maybe you don't know this love of Jesus as I do. Maybe you have never experienced His forgiving power. I have paraphrased the beautiful hymn, *Softly and Tenderly*,[7] in my own words. May the words of this song not allow you to rest until you get it right.

> So softly and tenderly Jesus is calling, He is calling not only for me but for you. He is always watching and waiting for you and waiting for me. He is ready for you to come home as He so tenderly calls us by our name. We have sinned and messed up that He washes white as snow, but He is ready for you to come home and lavish you with the love that He has promised. I know you are weary of fighting this back and forth, He is

---

[7] "Softly and Tenderly Jesus Is Calling," Softly and Tenderly Jesus Is Calling - HymnSite.com - United Methodist Hymnal #348, accessed December 19, 2020, https://www.hymnsite.com/lyrics/umh348.sht.

calling. His mercies are new and

waiting. All we need to do is answer His

voice and come home.

So, my friend, you and I can experience the

beauty of reuniting with our Heavenly Father

one day. It is not too late. The world is waiting

for you.

Help others come home.

Tregelles, Samuel P. *Gesenius' Hebrew-Chaldee Lexicon*. Grand Rapids, MI: Eerdmans, 1964.

About the Author

Valerie Millsapps, Director of the Pregnancy Resource Center in Maryville, TN, boldly encourages other Christians to step into their calling, and many times that is also being champions for the unborn. Valerie has had the opportunity to share on TBN'S the Huckabee show, B97.5 with Michelle Silva, Save the Storks Stork Ball, and many churches, businesses and small groups in East Tennessee. She would love to come share with you. To book Valerie to speak or if you would like more information, go to: www.valeriemillsapps.com

Made in the USA
Middletown, DE
24 July 2021